AFRICAN AMERICAN INTELLECTUAL-ACTIVISTS

Legacies in the Struggle

I0879149

DIA N.R. SEKAYI

Routledge
Taylor & Francis Group
NEW YORK AND LONDON

Published by Routledge
711 Third Avenue, New York, NY 10017
2 Park Square, Milton Park, Abingdon, Oxfordshire OX14 4RN
First issued in paperback 2014

Routledge is an imprint of the Taylor and Francis Group, an informa business

Transferred to Digital Printing 2010

Library of Congress Cataloging-in-Publication Data

Sekayi, Dia N.R.
African American intellectual-activists : legacies in the struggle / Dia N.R. Sekayi.
p. cm. — (Studies in African American history and culture)
Includes bibliographical references and index.
ISBN 978-0-8153-2921-3 (hbk)
ISBN 978-1-138-00174-9 (pbk)
1. Afro-American intellectuals—Interviews. 2. Afro-American intellectuals—Biography. 3. Political activists—United States—Interviews. 4. Political activists—United States—Biography. 5. Afro-Americans—Civil rights—History—20th century. 6. Black nationalism—United States—History—20th century. 7. Self-perception. I. Title. II. Series.
E185.86.S45 1997
323.1'196073—dc21 97-24279

Publisher's Note
The publisher has gone to great lengths to ensure the quality of this reprint but points out that some imperfections in the original may be apparent.

Contents

Foreword

by Mwalimu J. Shujaa

In *African American Intellectual Activists: Legacies in the Struggle,* Professor Dia Sekayi uses narrated life histories to introduce us to 11 women and men who are individually known and respected for their commitment and dedication to the uplift of African people. These men and women compel our attention because they have chosen a path in life that often brings them into conflict with the politically dominant culture in the United States. The respect they receive from others is earned because it is generally understood that one does pay a price for engaging in activism on behalf of African people. Through their own words and with the assistance of Professor Sekayi's insightful analyses, we learn how these African American intellectuals weigh the risks they take as activists and why they place such high value on the goals they are working to achieve.

The people who shared their life histories with Professor Sekayi maintain close affiliations with the pan-African nationalist community in the United States, although, as she points out, not all would identify themselves as nationalists. Professor Sekayi observes, however, that all of these men and women "agreed to some extent in the tenets of Black Nationalism." African Americans who struggle for self-determination and national liberation are also struggling against white supremacy and racism. Frantz Fanon (1983) warned us that the object of racism, as a form of cultural aggression, is not the individual African but the African "form of existing." Virtually every person of African descent who has experienced western schooling -- whether it be in Africa, Europe or North America -- knows this well. The pathway to becoming an intellectual in the western tradition takes one through the schooling process which, if not vigorously resisted, will most assuredly alienate any African from an appreciation of and respect for African forms of existing.

To fully appreciate *African American Intellectual Activists: Legacies in the Struggle*, one needs to understand that societal institutions in the United States are not intended to produce people who commit their lives to engaging in activism that challenges the cultural and political authority maintained by the nation state's ruling elite. Indeed, if one is regarded as an intellectual, s/he is expected to demonstrate some command of the intellectual history and paradigms of Europeans including European concepts of who Africans have been, are or should be. For those of us who have experienced this cultural assault, re-centering ourselves in African cultural history means consciously re-evaluating both our acquired knowledge bases and the interpretative frameworks we use to understand reality. Amilcar Cabral (1973) referred to this phenomenon as "re-Africanization." He described it as a "conversion of mind." The images presented in *African American Intellectual Activists: Legacies in the Struggle* help us to understand the dynamics of the purposeful personal transformation Cabral describes as it occurs among men and women of African descent in the United States.

Some time ago, Professor Marimba Ani (1980) began using the term Maafa ("disaster" in Kiswahili) to refer to the "trade in African lives and enslavement of African beings" as well as the continuing effects of this great tragedy on African people. Alienation from consciousness of ourselves as African beings is one of the wounds inflicted by the Maafa. In spite of the cultural oppression we experience, we know that there have been many times when we Africans recovering from the effects of enslavement and colonization have been able to tear ourselves away from the European-centered consciousness that engulfs our intelligence. As Fanon has told us, this tearing away is the only way to save ourselves from rootlessness. The first determination that must be made in our analysis of the tearing away process is to identify what compels an African to look for a way to liberate his/her consciousness. Too many of us who are "conceptually incarcerated" (see Nobles, 1986) do not seek freedom from this condition because our notions about who Africans are in the world have been learned through the institutions that maintain white supremacy by inculcating ideas of African inferiority. A person who doesn't realize s/he is lost is not looking for a way home.

While the Maafa has been a collective experience for us as Africans, we have each lived it in personal contexts, as well. Therefore, we each have to overcome our personal challenges in order to make the choices necessary to change the way we live. Some of us remain yoked to

STUDIES IN

AFRICAN AMERICAN HISTORY AND CULTURE

edited by

GRAHAM RUSSELL HODGES
COLGATE UNIVERSITY

A GARLAND SERIES

alien realities because they are the only realities we know. This is one of the most tragic effects of the Maafa. Nkrumah recognized this and it is what led him to say that "the secret of life is to have no fear." We must individually overcome our fear of what we do not know. We can be aided in the process, but, ultimately, it is as individuals that we must make the decision to let go of our fear. Sometimes what is feared is the action that one may be compelled to take as a consequence of what one knows.

Professor Sekayi is driven to understand why, out of life's myriad roads, these men and women chose to be intellectual activists. Knowing her as I do, it is not ironic that her own life history is emblematic of African people's ongoing struggle to reclaim knowledge of ancestral wisdom from an alienation imposed by epochs of enslavement and colonization. Her presentation of these stories is sensitive to the need to reclaim cultural memory she shares with the women and men whose stories she tells in this book. This is an important work. It will stand as a contribution to the recorded history of the African experience.

References

Ani (Richards), Marimba (1980). *Let the Circle be Unbroken: The Implications of African Spirituality in the Diaspora*. Trenton, NJ: The Red Sea Press

Cabral, Amilcar. (1973). "National Liberation and Culture." In Africa Information Service (Ed.) *Return to the Source: Selected Speeches by Amilcar Cabral*. New York: Monthly Review Press, 39-56

Fanon, Frantz. (1983). *The Wretched of the Earth*. New York: Penguin (Published originally in 1961 as *Les Damnés de la Terre*).

Nobles, Wade W. (1986). *African Psychology: Toward Its Reclamation, Raeacension and Revitalization*. Oakland: The Institute for Advanced Study of Black Family Life and Culture.

Acknowledgements

I would like to offer my most sincere thanks to all of the people in my life who have supported me in the completion of this book. I offer my appreciation to all of the activists who shared their lives with me and made this book possible. I would like to express my gratitude to my mentor, Mwalimu Shujaa, who helped me to open my mind to all kinds of possibilities; a gift that keeps on giving. My thanks and respect to my best friend Kimberly Davis, with whom I've philosophized for nearly 20 years on subjects great and small. To my other best friend David Simmons with whom I've shared an incredibly symbiotic friendship for the past 7 years, thank you. To Steve Thomas, a dandelion. To Monique Davis and Angela Exum-Ferary, for believing in my ability. To my oldest friends from Riley street; Lynda, Lynette, Avis, Joey and Bernell, much love. To all those with whom I've shared intellectual debate; Nicole, Yvette, Tracy, Brian, Ken, Kimberly A., Lin, Lindiwe, Ramla and Margaret, just to name a few. And finally to my parents, Laura Ballard and Joseph Ballard who always seem to accept my intellectual abilities without question, I write to you now what I wrote to you in my high school yearbook 12 years ago "Please be patient with me, God isn't through with me yet. But when God gets through with me, I shall come forth as pure gold !"

Dia Sekayi, 1997

African American Intellectual-Activists

I
Introduction

African-American nationalism (a form of activism) has been described as the belief in the right of all African people in America to total self-determination in every aspect of life. In my experience, African-American nationalists understand that the achievement of this goal will come only as a result of struggle. My study delves into the lives of 11 people who are closely affiliated with the African-American nationalist community. Initially I assumed, because of their close relationships with the nationalist community, that all would welcome the African-American nationalist title. As I proceeded with the interviews, I discovered that my initial assumption was faulty. Therefore, this study became not one of self-proclaimed African-American nationalists, but rather one African-American intellectual-activists who maintain close ties and partnerships with the nationalist community.

Activism is defined in Webster's New World Dictionary as taking a direct action to achieve a political or social end. My purpose was to discover what makes each of these activists tick, why they are who they are and most importantly, how they came to be who they are.

The issue of responsibility is key in my study. Personal experience and my own sense of responsibility to my community are the real motivations for the choice of this topic. In the all African-American community where I grew up, activities such as studying diligently, enjoying school, reading outside of school and other intellectually motivated activities were looked down upon. Jawanza Kunjufu (1988) discusses the perception held by many young African-Americans that a choice needs to be made about whether to be popular or smart. Fordham and Ogbu (1986) discuss how excelling academically is often seen as "acting white." They go on to discuss the internal conflict that occurs when an individual crosses what he or she sees as a cultural boundary by working to do well in school. This concept certainly played itself out when I was growing up and still exists today, with alarming strength, among young African-Americans. This is evident from my experiences teaching African-American junior high school students at a public neighborhood school. The attitudes of the students, especially the males, was generally that studying, doing homework and participating in classroom activities are things that are considered "nerdy" and "white."

As a result of my experiences, I began to think very seriously about what kind of role I could play in alleviating this misconception that to be "smart" is to be "white" and therefore unpopular. As I analyzed this situation, I realized that if this misconception persisted among young African-Americans, we as a community may face a shortage of intellectuals in the next generation. If children and young adults were hesitant about being serious critical thinkers, how would they ever discover the concept of African-American nationalism or for that matter, activism of any sort. Who would carry on the struggle for the self-determination that is, in my opinion, necessary to the health and well being of the African-American community. Someone, some group of African-Americans must assume the responsibility for motivating the next generation. Someone, some group needs to do more than just engage in intellectual dialogue. The observations that I have made of school-aged African-Americans has certainly reinforced for me the importance of praxis: the combination of intellect, or thought, and action (Freire, 1970).

It is imperative that something be done to encourage the development of a new generation of African-American intellectual-nationalists. It is simply not enough to be an intellectual. Intellectualism without action is, in my opinion, worthless. And, activism without informed, critical thinking can result in impulsiveness with few or no lasting effects. An example of the latter combination is the current popularity of slain African-American nationalist, Malcolm X. The present fad is to wear the "X" hat, a symbol of a movie based upon the life of Malcolm X, or a variety of tee shirts with pictures of Malcolm labeled with various catchy phrases and out of context quotes such as, "by any means necessary." Many of the individuals who proudly wear Malcolm X paraphernalia have never read his autobiography or other writings by or about him and have little sense of the philosophies of this man. Hopefully, some of these individuals will be moved to study, but as stated earlier, this "activism" without critical, informed thought will likely have few or no lasting effects.

The challenge, then, is to enrich the "activism" by infusing knowledge and critical thinking skills. Many people in American society are taught facts and memorization skills. This can contribute to miseducation. A true and lasting education teaches people *how* to think, not *what* to think. This is an essential point to understand when discussing the issue of education versus miseducation, and is one to which I will continually refer. When a group of people constitute a numerical minority in a society, with little political power over their own lives, it is extremely important that they learn how to think. The majority population will likely have the most influence on how members in that society are educated and it would be logical for them to structure an educational system most beneficial to their needs. It is up to the various "minority" populations to educate their own in ways that are most conducive to their survival and uplift. Over time, African-Americans have used education as a way of escaping the oppression they are subjected to within American society. Many African-Americans have concluded that there is a problem with how they and their offspring have been and are being educated.

The Problem and Its Background

This research has been guided by the following questions: what in the lives of the individuals in this study led each of them to become activists? Further, are there common themes in their narrated life experiences that have motivated their activism?

In a paper published in 1973, E. Franklin Frazier criticized African-American intellectuals for "integration mania," intellectual sterility and ideological submissiveness. He asserted that African-American intellectuals of his time were so concerned with the possibility of integration and eventual assimilation that they were not as focused, as he felt they should have been, on issues regarding the quality of life for the African-American masses (Frazier, 1973).

Frazier's criticism of African-American intellectuals was deduced from his assessment of the formal education they received. He argued that African-American educational institutions did not grow out of the traditional culture of the African-American people. Moreover, Frazier contended that the schools maintained by the free Africans in America were both the result of and part of the process of assimilating European culture. He added that "while the first generation of Negro teachers who gradually replaced the early white teachers enjoyed considerable prestige among Negro masses, they too were in a sense representatives of the white man's way of life" (pg. 96). That this contingent of African-American teachers was perceived to be hardly different from white teachers in what and how it taught African-Americans about the superiority of western culture is an example of what can result from miseducation.

I define miseducation as a combination of formal schooling and life experiences that is designed to benefit some person or group of people other than the person or group that is being taught. Woodson (1933) talked about how the "mis-education" of the formally educated African-American left him/her unequipped to serve the "uneducated masses." He says, of the mis-educated African-American that:

> . . . for the arduous task of serving a race thus handicapped, however, the Negro has had little or no training at all. The people whom he has been ordered to serve have been belittled by his teachers to the extent that he can hardly find delight in what his education has led him to think is impossible. (pg. 6)

Woodson's comment implies that even some of the African-Americans who have been formally educated and work in African-American communities can be so profoundly miseducated that they may see their own race as hopeless.

Akbar's (1982) writings support the notion that there has been gross miseducation of African-Americans. He discusses the difference between a true education, which he defines as "knowing thyself," and mere training. He goes on to say that until African-Americans begin to know themselves individually, tribally (as a community), and spiritually, there will be little or no progress for them as a people.

Here we have three African-American intellectuals, Frazier, Woodson and Akbar, writing over a time span of 50 years, who each discuss the same phenomenon of miseducation and its detrimental effects on the African-American community. Moreover, they each discuss the responsibility of African-American intellectuals to identify with and commit themselves to the uplift of the African-American masses. Thus, some of the concerns that guide my research relate to learning more about what motivates these African-American intellectuals to commit themselves to the uplift of the masses.

I am also interested in the progression from "common man" to intellectual-activist; in other words, personal transformation The intellectual is distinguished by his or her formal schooling. Thus, I define an intellectual as an individual whose formal education along with his or her life experiences have left them with a body of knowledge, to which they are continually adding, on a variety of subjects matter. In the context of this study, an intellectual-activist is one who works regularly on behalf of or has made a career of uplifting the African-American race.

Freire (1970) describes a process in which an individual moves from semi-intransitivity of consciousness to naive transitivity to the critical transitivity of consciousness. These categories trace an individuals' development of consciousness from being concerned only with things that are biologically necessary for survival to a stage where other problems are recognized, but over-simplified to finally a stage where problems and situations of all sorts are acknowledged and considered seriously and critically.

Freire's description is useful, however, Asante (1988) describes a progression toward critical consciousness more specific to the African-American experience. He describes five levels awareness that lead to personal transformation toward a level of consciousness called

"Afrocentricity." ***Skin recognition*** is the first level that occurs when a person recognizes that his or her skin or heritage is black, but is unable to carry that any further. ***Environmental recognition*** occurs when an individual sees the environment as indicating his or her Blackness through discrimination and abuse. ***Personality Awareness*** happens when a person professes to like things that are stereotypically African-American, such as food, music or dance. ***Interest-concern*** is the fourth level and occurs when an individual "accepts the first three levels and demonstrates interest and concern in the problems of Blacks and tries to deal intelligently with the issues of the African people. The fifth level, ***Afrocentric awareness***, occurs when the individual "becomes totally changed to a conscious level of involvement in the struggle for his or her own mind liberation" (pg. 49).

Asante's analysis raises additional questions that are relevant to this research. To the extent that the 11 intellectual-activists who participated in this study classify themselves as Afrocentric, did they experience a process like that described by Asante? Can the experiences that lead individuals to become intellectual-activists be categorized? Finally, can these categories be used to assist other African-Americans in reaching that "vantage ground," as idealized by DuBois (1969) with regard to the "talented tenth"? This research seeks to describe the particular events or gradual progression, as articulated by the interviewees, that led to each one's critical cultural awareness, an awareness that moved them to go beyond intellectualism to their current states as intellectual-activists.

The progression to intellectual-activism is as important as the actual state of intellectual-activism, when the intellectual goes beyond simply thinking, analyzing and evaluating different concepts, issues and situations to taking physical steps to convert thoughts into action. This is similar to Freire's concept of transitive consciousness which involves the critical acknowledgment and consideration of various problems and situations. Friere's (1970) concept of praxis, in which an individual converts reflection into action or, put another way, converts word into work, is relevant to the discussion of intellectual-activism. He writes that when action is sacrificed, you are left with "verbalism" and when reflection is sacrificed, you are left with "activism." I have interpreted activism as it is used by Friere to mean impulsive actions taken before any critical, analytical or evaluative thought or discussion took place on the issue that was acted upon.

Significance

Although research is important, the practical application of that research is even more important. My main question of what in the life of a nationalist makes the individual that way, is asked for practical reasons.

It is possible that if we can pinpoint some of the factors within the lives of nationalists that have brought them to this state, that we may be able to reproduce those factors into the lives of others. For example, if high self esteem and positive role models are the factors that are common to the lives of the African-American nationalists that are being studied here, programs could be developed within and by the African-American community that focus on building self esteem while providing positive role models.

It is my intention to continue this research to a level at which I might be able to pinpoint some of those common threads to as great an extent as is possible. It is important that the African-American community produces young people who are socially conscious, in a sense that they know what's going on, and socially active, in a sense that they are moved to do something about it. Those are the most important things. The African-American community will only be liberated through revolution. And as Che Guevara and others have said; there can be no revolution without love; love of one's self, of one's people and of freedom.

II
Literature Review

Definitions

The next three sections will cover the qualifications that various scholars have given for being considered an intellectual or an activist. Throughout I will incorporate critical evaluations of their definitions and my own definitions for the purpose of this study.

The concept of an intellectual has been given many meanings over time based on many different criteria. Often the basis is connected with formal education. Anyone whose schooling has gone beyond high school could be considered an intellectual. The cut off point can be adjusted according to the average level of education in a given society or culture, with anything above average being considered intellectual. It can be broken down even further within the realm of formal education by field or area of study. Although a medical doctor would certainly be considered "smart" or knowledgeable by most people, a college professor may more often be considered "intellectual." Perhaps because he or she makes a living in an educational setting and a continuous increasing of knowledge is implied.

Hare's (1973) definition of a scholar is similar to the many definitions given of intellectual; he writes that a scholar is a person who contributes original ideas, new insights and information to the existing fund of knowledge—whether or not he has a string of academic degrees or executes his scholarly activities in a manner appropriate to the traditions and conventions of the existing world of scholarship. He goes further to write that Black scholars will provide the catalysts not only for Black liberation but perhaps for the ultimate resolution of America's pathology now infecting, in some form or fashion, the entire world.

I distinguish the "formally educated" from the "intellectual" on the basis of what happens with an individual *after* the completion of formal schooling. The participants in this study have continued to engage in scholarly pursuits after and outside of formal schooling. Intellectuals are critical thinkers and intellectual progress continues when critical thinking continues. To further illustrate, if one was formally educated in the 1930s but did not update his or her education by continually rethinking new situations and new issues, could that individual be considered a present-day intellectual?

The distinction then, between an "intellectual" and someone who is simply "formally educated" will be the continuation of the intellectual activity, the constant state of thinking, analyzing and evaluating different concepts, issues and situations inside and outside of the traditional educational setting. In the next section I will discuss the issue of education, miseducation and the importance of these two concepts for the uplift of African-American people.

Education Versus Miseducation

The issue to be addressed in this section is the fundamental difference between the African-American intellectual who feels a strong obligation towards activism and the one who neither feels the obligation nor cares one way or the other about activism. It has been said by several different scholars and laypersons, that the difference is the kind of education one receives. Kinds of education can be broken down into two main categories; true education and miseducation.

Woodson (1933) wrote about the miseducation that the African-American has been subjected to by others and his own. His definition includes nearly every aspect of life. I would add ideas, culture and values as other aspects of life that people are trained to respect. Respecting only the ideas, culture and values of others can also contribute to miseducation, which can be detrimental not only to individual African-Americans, but to the race as a whole. Woodson comments on this when he writes:

> The selfish struggle for personal aggrandizement, which has not yet brought either faction more than an appointment on the police force or

> a clerkship in one of the city offices, thus blocks the social and economic progress of thousands of unoffending people. (pg. 113)

This issue is important because it is an illustration that just because one or two African-Americans "make it," does not necessarily mean that the problems of the race have been solved and thus undeserving of any further attention.

E. Franklin Frazier (1973) also wrote on the miseducation of the African-American as it relates to the failure of the African-American intellectual. He wrote that " . . . with the few exceptions of literary men, it appears that the Negro intellectual is unconscious of the extent to which his thinking is restricted to sterile repetition of the safe and conventional ideas current in American society." He went on to write that " . . . the educated Negro or Negro intellectuals have failed to achieve any intellectual freedom (pg. 59)." I have interpreted each of these statements as discussing the issue of true education versus miseducation. The African-American that he speaks of in the first quote has a great deal of formal education, thus he is labeled an intellectual. However, this man has been taught what to think, not how to think. This issue is being addressed in the second quote; a man can posses a formal higher education without attaining intellectual freedom. Intellectual freedom is the ability to think independently of "acceptable" issues in society. The next issue to be addressed is that of the relationship between the African-American intellectuals and the African-American masses.

The Relationship Between African-American Intellectuals and the African-American Masses

The often strained relationship between African-American intellectuals and the African-American masses may be related to the miseducation to which African-Americans in general have traditionally been exposed. Woodson (1933) devoted an entire book to the discussion of the miseducation of African-Americans.

Woodson describes miseducation as training that teaches people to respect the knowledge, the scholarship, the history and the background of everyone except themselves. His definition describes what is happening in contemporary American society. For example, an individual can attain the highest academic or professional degree in the field of education, (Ph.D. or Ed.D, respectively), without being *required* to study any African-American authors. In a society where 12 per cent of the population is African-American (and a much higher percentage of the public school enrollment across the country is made up of African-Americans), the total absence or limited presence of African-American scholars in the curriculum is inappropriate and unacceptable. The importance of studying African-American issues through the eyes and minds of African-Americans is twofold. On one hand, and most importantly, these scholars possess information that is crucial to the academic community (and the community at large), and secondly, people grow tired of being told how they feel, how they should be dealt with and approached and what is important to them by people other than themselves. (In other words, people *do* tire of being mis-educated.)

Akbar (1982) uses an analogy involving a dog. He writes that when a dog learns how to bury bones and to hunt more effectively for meat to feed himself and his family—that dog is educated. He goes on to say that when a dog learns how to stand on its two hind legs and wear a dress and dance to music—that dog is simply trained. Using Woodson's terms, the latter dog is learning to respect what humans consider knowledge (and entertainment). How useful is this aspect of human knowledge for a dog? It may, in fact, be considered detrimental since the time spent mastering this "human knowledge" is time taken away from the potential mastery of "dog knowledge." So what then is the remedy for mis-education? And what lies at the other end of the spectrum?

A real education is defined as having real knowledge. Akbar (1982) wrote that those who have been in search of knowledge have been told by the great powers of the world that **knowledge of self is the source of real knowledge**. I will base my definition of a real education upon "knowledge of self." Asante (1988) stresses the importance of the transformation to a true consciousness. This true consciousness and awareness of self are sources of real knowledge. The final step of the transformation, according to Asante is "Afrocentric Awareness."

Jackson and Hardiman (1983) also discuss steps to identity formation. Stage one is acceptance: "white is right." Stage two is resistance: the individual challenges and rejects acceptance consciousness. Stage three is redefinition: the individual shifts energies towards other African-Americans. And stage four is internalization: a redefined sense of Blackness.

Identity formation and concept of self are key to overcoming mis-education and achieving a real education, which will constantly be compared to and contrasted with mis-education. In American society, a much higher value is placed on having knowledge that is respected by European Americans. If the larger society cannot provide a real education for African-Americans (and in fact, it is not desirable for one group to teach another how to "know themselves") then it is the responsibility of those African-Americans who possess a true education to share it with the masses. This sharing could take many forms such as reorganizing the community and providing alternative educational programs for the masses. This segment of the society is the intellectual segment. Over the years, the shortcomings of the African-American intellectual have been analyzed and reanalyzed. The responsibilities of this segment of the African-American population have been laid out in great detail by African-American philosophers, sociologists, educators and popular writers.

W.E.B. DuBois discussed what he saw as the responsibilities of the "talented tenth" of African-Americans. He argued that educated men and women have a duty to look out for the interests of the masses. He wrote that:

> Progress in human affairs is more often a *pull* than a push, a surging forward of the exceptional man, and the lifting of his duller brethren slowly and painfully to his vantage ground. (DuBois, 1969, pg.78)

This statement illustrates DuBois' idea that those African-Americans who excel have a responsibility pull up those who have not, to a more desirable place in society. (Although DuBois' statements may seem somewhat elitist, the concept of the talented tenth and the responsibilities therein were developed for the purpose of the uplift of the race. DuBois was operating from his own reality, which is what many philosophers and people in general do, and apparently, from his experiences, the "exceptional" men were the most equipped to facilitate change. (In fact, DuBois later rejected the notion that only a small segment of the African-American community were responsible for change.)

Duties and Responsibilities of the Intellectual

In reviewing the literature on the duties and responsibilities of the African-American intellectual, I found that there is much agreement among African-American scholars.

DuBois (1969) wrote that not only African-Americans, but all races will be saved by its exceptional men. He further wrote that it is important to develop the best of the race because it is their responsibility to guide the masses away from the negative, deadly aspects of all the races, including their own. DuBois is clearly communicating his belief that a small segment of the African-American community is responsible for the well-being of the majority. (Again, he later rejects this notion). He comments that the two historic mistakes that have hindered human progress are the thinking first that no more could ever rise save the few already risen; or second, that it would be better the unrisen pull the risen down. This point is key to this research because these two mistakes are still being made. The African-American masses often see intellectuals as "up there" at a point that is unattainable for them. They may see these intellectuals as possessing qualities that they neither have nor have the ability to attain. Additionally, there is a segment of the community who will not be satisfied until they have brought down those who have struggled to rise up. This summarizes at least part of the historical context of the struggles of the African-American intellectuals; against groups both inside and outside of the culture.

Cruse (1967), raises many important points with regard to the role the African-American intellectual should play. He writes that "the Negro intellectual must deal intimately with the white power structure and cultural apparatus and the inner realities of the Black world at one and the same time" (pg. 459). DuBois (1961) discussion of double-counsciousness is relevant here. This is a most difficult role to play successfully. How does one individual become so closely involved with the white power structure in America without "selling out" the African-American masses. It may even be deemed impossible.

While living in the United States of America, it would be a difficult task to completely divorce oneself from the white majority in society. The African-American intellectual is equipped to develop a strategy to become involved without alienating his or her own people. This is the role that Cruse (1967) challenges the intellectual to play when he argues that the African-American intellectual *must* learn how one might control and channel such political, social and economic forces. Cruse goes on to say that " . . . the functional role of the Negro intellectual demands that he *cannot* be absolutely separated from either the Black or white world" (pg. 452). Again, playing this role and playing it well is truly one of the crises of the African-American intellectual. Playing it well consists of functioning in white society while uplifting the African-American masses.

Many times though, the intellectual alienates one or the other group, the middle class white intellectuals or the African-American masses. When she alienates the latter, she would be referred to as an "oreo"; black on the outside, white on the inside. When the former is alienated, it has been referred to as "class suicide."

The concept of class suicide was first discussed by Marx (1948) and later put into an African-American context by Karenga (1985), who begins by addressing the responsibilities of the African-American intellectual. He writes:

> There is the continuing concession that this class is most conscious of the possibilities of change and that a segment of this class must accept the historical responsibility of imbuing the masses with a new active self consciousness which will culminate in self liberation. (Karenga, pg. 91)

Karenga's analysis is relevant because he discusses the duties of the middle class intellectual with regard to self liberation. (Note that Karenga, like Frazier and others, assume that the African-American intellectual is almost by definition, middle class.) Karenga differs from DuBois in that he sees the responsibility as helping the masses to help themselves, whereas DuBois , at least initially, put more emphasis on the middle class uplifting the masses. Class suicide and where the courage to "commit" it comes from is one of the fundamental questions being asked in this research.

Karenga refers to Lenin and Gramsci as having similar ideas on the role of the intellectual. He charges intellectuals with "the decisive role in the theoretical and practical project of liberation, grasping the fundamental dimensions of the situation and developing strategies and structures to change it" (pg.91).

The roles and responsibilities of the African-American intellectual have been well laid out over the years. The main responsibility being to maintain a relationship with the larger African-American community for the purpose of uplifting the race. Some emphasize helping the masses to help themselves while some give the responsibility of racial uplift primarily to the intellectual. Many African-American intellectuals agree with and carry out the responsibilities assigned to them. But what happens in the lives of those who chose not to? Many of those who agree with the responsibilities assigned to the intellectuals say that those who do not must have experienced a "miseducation" so potent that they were unable to rise above it.

West and Hooks (1991) discuss the attitudes of the African-American community towards its intellectuals. They write that "in addition to the general anti-intellectual tenor of American society, there is a deep distrust and suspicion of the Black community toward Black intellectuals" (pg. 134). They site the most important cause of this attitude as the "widespread refusal of Black intellectuals to remain, in some visible way, organically linked with Afro-American cultural life" (pg. 134). This strained relationship is one of the results of miseducation.

The issue of "miseducation" has been discussed by many scholars; most memorably by Carter G. Woodson in his 1933 work, *The Miseducation of the Negro*. Beverly Gordon (1990), who draws heavily on Woodson, discusses the necessity of African-American epistemology for educational theory and practice. She writes about the marginalization of the African-American perspective in "dominant literature." Gordon's work is extremely important because it forces us to reanalyze the quality of an educational system that minimizes the work of an entire race of people. This study is based in part upon Dr. Gordon's calling for an African-American epistemology. An African-American theory of knowledge is represented here through the stories of these African-Americanintellectual-activists. Crucial to the concept of African-American epistemology are the voices of African-Americans themselves. This is a beginning to breaking down the walls of miseducation.

Woodson's definition of miseducation and Gordon's discussion of the marginalization of the work of African-American scholars make an excellent argument that African-Americans have all been miseducated at one point or another during their formal schooling.

The way in which miseducation has contributed to the failure of the African-American intellectual will be discussed in the next section.

Failure of the African-American Intellectual

Whenever responsibilities are assigned to an individual or group of people, a time will come when that individual or group will be judged as to whether or not they have been successful at meeting these responsibilities. People are not always praised for simply living up to responsibilities. This is the minimum that is expected and often no recognition is given. However, when failure occurs, much is heard, said and written about the situation. The failure (or the perceived failure) of the African-American intellectual is no exception.

In order to label the African-American intellectual a failure, a discussion about the unmet expectations must take place.

Harold Cruse (1967) writes about the failure of the African-American intellectual in terms of a crisis. The crisis occurs when theintellectual is unable to successfully interact in the larger white society while simultaneously interacting among the African-American masses. A crisis is a crucial or critical situation. The crucial situation for the African-American community is related to the basic survival of the race. The African-American intellectual "elite" is in danger of identifying with their white counterparts. Cruse refers to those counterparts as " . . . intellectually bloated, dull, unoriginal, critically tongue-tied, smug (or downright scared), time serving and societally dishonest." (1967, pg.456) When Cruse's description of the white intellectual elite occurs among the African-American intellectual elite there is a societal effect that is a somewhat different than that among whites. If one buys into the concept of the "talented tenth," the assumption is that it is the responsibility of this segment of society to uplift the race. So, if this group becomes all of the things that the white elite is described as (by Cruse), a crisis will surely occur.

Woodson further commented on the effects of the lack of feeling of responsibility towards the less informed masses and how its ill effects are magnified when it occurs in the African-American community:

> This attitude of the educated Negro toward the masses results partly from the general trend of all persons toward selfishness, but it works more disastrously among the Negroes than among the whites because the lower classes of the latter have had so much more opportunity. (1933, pg. 56)

Woodson makes a valid point. Considering the status of Africans in American society, I assert that we simply cannot afford to be selfish. When DuBois' talented tenth become selfish, the whole race suffers since the expectation is that they uplift the masses. I disagree with the talented tenth concept to a certain extent. In fact, DuBois reassesses his own philosophy. I believe that far more that ten per cent of the race has the ability to be self-motivated enough to uplift the race. The construction worker or the plumber or the home health care aide who reads or understands the needs of the African-American race from their own personal experience, are just as qualified to contribute to the uplift. I believe that the African-American intellectual is made, not born and can be drawn from any segment of society.

Frazier (1973) has also written a great deal on the failure of the African-American intellectual. He has commented on why and how they have failed. He writes that the African-American intellectual is unable to recognize the importance of the American enslavement experience because he continues to be an unconscious victim of these experiences. Here Frazier speaks of an issue that is very fundamental to the success or failure of the race as a whole and to individuals within it; the ability or inability to overcome miseducation. The enslavement experience involved massive amounts of miseducation; in the form of a religion that justified the situation, daily training that promoted low self image and the general brainwashing that told the enslaved that they were not whole persons. The American enslavement of Africans is probably one of the best examples of miseducation.

Frazier not only discusses why African-American intellectuals have failed, but also the ways in which they have failed. He writes about the way they have failed to study the problems of African-Americans in a manner which would place their fate in the broad framework of man's experience in this world and that they have engaged in petty defenses of their social failures. Frazier, however, does not necessarily *blame* the intellectual for his failures because he writes that this class emerged by virtue of white American philanthropy. Again, another way of saying that the African-American intellectual has failed, in large part, because of miseducation.

Summary

My literature review revealed a great deal of interesting and relevant work an the area of the history and present African-American intellectuals. A variety of definitions for what it means to be an African-American intellectual were discovered. The issues of education versus miseducation, the relationship between African-American intellectuals and the African-American masses, the duties and responsibilities of the African-American intellectual and the failure therein were raised and discussed.

The concept of miseducation was studied by a variety of people. The definition of miseducation, the cause and problems resulting from miseducation was a common and important theme. Additionally, the concept of African-American intellectual was approached from a variety perspectives, including the history and definition, the relationship between them and the general African-American public, the perceived "responsibilities" of and the failure to meet these "responsibilities."

Further, the concept of the African-American intellectual-activist was discussed. The literature revealed that most of the discussion focussed on the *fact* that intellectual-activists *exist*, the mental, physical and emotional processes that occurred while they *became* activists, in other words, their transformation to the state of intellectual-activist is what interests me and drives this research.

III
Methodology

Conceptual Framework

West (1990) argues that "the choice of becoming a Black intellectual is an act of self-imposed marginality; it assures a peripheral status in and to the Black community" (pg 132). My view is similar to West's in that intellectuals are made and not born. West goes on to discuss the reasons why African-Americans chose to become serious intellectuals. He writes that the reasons are diverse "but in most cases, the reasons can be traced back to a common root: a conversion-like experience with a highly influential teacher or peer that convinced one to dedicate ones life to the activities of reading, writing and conversing for the purposes of individual pleasure, personal growth and political enhancement of Black (and often other oppressed) people" (pg.132).

West's notion of a "common root" can be discerned in Alex Haley's *Autobiography of Malcolm X*. When Malcolm was in prison, he had an encounter with a fellow prisoner who spoke to him about the Nation of Islam. This encounter changed the course of his entire life. Malcolm's situation is just one example that illustrates West's theory about a conversion-like experience. This is a useful point for the purpose of practical application. Analyzing these types of experiences as they have occurred in the lives of others will be helpful when working to motivate young people.

I decided that the best way to study the life of an intellectual activist is tolisten to the life story directly from that person. In this study, I interviewed African-American individuals whose activism takes place in the context of nationalism. My study revolved around nationalists for several reasons. The primary reason is that the individuals that I interviewed are people that are making positive things happen in the African-American community. The approach that they have traditionally taken has worked and is still working. I wanted to study their lives so that when they are gone, we will be able to replenish the nationalist community with today's children. All of the interviewees do not have advanced college degrees, but the body of knowledge held by each of them is astounding. They are, in my mind, the true intellectuals. Through study, both formal and informal, and life experiences they have developed an attitude, or more appropriately, a way of life that is affecting the African-American community in an amazing way. Walter Rodney (1990) writes:

> And when people reach close to the top they find that a) there is no room within the society and b) there is a greater salability [elsewhere] of those skills which they have learned because, having become a commodity, they can rise up in the commodity market which is wider than Guyana . . . therefore the best of our people have traditionally just reached a certain point and just moved out through the conduits that lead out of our society. (pg. 3)

Although Rodney writes of people of African descent in Guyana, the same might be said of a contingent of African-Americans. The point among my peers had always been the issue of "making it out of here." The ideal situation was going to college, doing well and moving on. This was not only accepted by people in the family, it was desired. Rodney (1990) speaks to this:

> . . . for some very often their parents and their families are quite pleased about this. They are quite pleased to say we have such and such a son who is a doctor in Ontario, Canada. But needless to say, he isn't curing any disease in Guyana. (pg. 3)

Each of my participants have made a conscious choice continue to work in the community despite the option, for most of them, to divorce themselves completely in favor of more lucrative opportunities. Even though all of the participants are not employed full time by community institutions, all focus their energies on issues of concern to the African-American community through their work. I would like to find out how and why they came to make this choice.

Life History Approach

The life history approach is an in depth look at the experiences of an individual or a group of people as delivered orally by the people themselves. There are several different types of life histories according to Denzin (1970): the complete life history, the topical life history and the edited life history. My research reflects a modified combination of the topical and edited types. The major modification was in the length of the interview sessions. In many cases, a life history study includes multiple interviews over a period of time. For the purpose of the timely completion of this study, only one formal interview was conducted.

The complete life history covers the entirety of an individual's life experiences. There are three features in the complete type that are shared in the topical type except in the latter, the focus is on only one aspect of the person's life. The three features are as follows: "the person's 'own story of his life', the social and cultural situation to which he and others see him responding and the sequence of past experiences and situations in his life" (pg. 230).

Finally, the edited life history consists of regular inclusion of "comments, explanations and questions by someone other than the focal subject" (Denzin, pg. 231) Again, my study reflects the topical and edited types of life history.

I chose this approach because of several factors: 1) at this point in the lives and careers of the 11 individuals being interviewed, they have a wealth of interesting information to share, 2) they each have the ability to reflect on many relevant events (ones that are the focus of this study) that have occurred within their lifetimes, 3) the individuals I have chosen are very articulate and seem to possess good memories and have lived through the kinds of experiences I am interested in studying and 4) they are still active and are able to talk about how what they have learned thus far is influencing their present and future plans. According to Bogdan and Biklen (1982), these qualities in an individual are ones that will determine the feasibility of doing a life history case study.

I selected my sample of 11 African-Americans primarily from the Chicago area. All 11 men and women maintain close ties with the African-American nationalist community.

My method of data collection was primarily in depth interviews with each member of the sample. Moss (1974) wrote that the most orthodox form of oral history is "an interview in which one person solicits from another his recollections and opinions of people, places events and concepts" (pg. 7). However, although "purists" might frown on it, other sources of information, such as diaries, legal records and articles, can be included in oral history. In the cases of 5 of the participants, I used information that they wrote about themselves or information written about them in books, articles or newspapers.

The interviews were aimed at documenting the relevant life experiences of the individuals participating in the study. Relevant experiences included any experiences that the interviewee considers to be important factors in the formation of their current statuses as activists within the context of nationalism.

A pilot study was conducted on two African-American nationalists in 1991. From this study emerged several categories that were useful to forming the questions for the current research. Those categories were 1) turning points, 2) life purposes, 3) experiences that influenced social consciousness and 4) self esteem.

The question asked in this research was what are the reasons individuals become activists in the form of nationalism as determined by the narrated life experiences of African-Americans who are nationalists. The way an individual lives his or her life is directly related to the experiences that individual endured over time. Those life directing experiences may have occurred within an educational setting, the home environment, the larger community or a religious setting.

The time spent in each initial interview was approximately two hours. Follow up, informal interviews were conducted with several of the participants, either by telephone or in person, for the purpose of clarification or to address topics not discussed in the initial interview. The total time spent with each participant was approximately three hours.

There were ten guiding questions. The number of questions asked and time taken for the interview varied depending on how the interview progressed. Some people needed only be given an overview of the study and talked continuously for an hour while others need more guidance and structure, in which case the interview may last two hours. After recording the interviews, all relevant parts of the tapes were transcribed. Sections of the tape such as interruptions or tangents to the conversations were not transcribed. Several of the participants expressed an interest in reading the transcripts of their interviews. These requests were accomodated. I found, however, that the comments made by the participants as a result of the reading of the transcripts were not always useful. On several occasions, participants wanted to reword or delete prior statements. In one case, an participant wanted to delete a key statement that I had intended to use in my analysis. As a matter of consideration, I honored the participant's request.

After transcription, I created categories that covered the discussion on what the interviewee felt contributed to his or her current status in the African-American nationalist community.

After those categories were established, they were grouped into fewer more general topics. The categories created from the pilot study were used as a general guide with which to begin. Wherever necessary, the categories were altered or deleted and new categories were added. The specific method of interviewing was based on work by Kesho Scott (1991), who did similar work on the life histories of African-American women. The interviewing style of general open ended questions asked for the purpose of motivating detailed, personal responses is a technique adapted from Scott.

The environment in which the nationalists were raised cannot be ignored as a factor that influenced their life choices. Environment includes the home, the school, the church, the immediate community and the larger community (i.e. the city). The personal interviews that were conducted included discussion on each of these environments.

Charlotte Linde (1989) states that the most important part of a narrative is the evaluation. She writes that " . . . the evaluative material adds the social dimension of what the events mean, which permits the interlocutors to create and negotiate their social meaning." (pg. 1) I attempted to negotiate the social meaning in the categories that emerged from the interview data.

Stanfield (1993) wrote about the challenges present when research takes place across race, class or gender lines. He asserts that even when researcher and subject are of the same race complications may still exist.

> The class gap between the researcher of color and subjects of color, who are more than likely poor as well as racially oppressed, is a particularly touchy issue for those who view themselves as liberators of the oppressed. (pg. 9)

Although I believe that Stanfield raises a valid point, because of the nature of my study, which is based on African-Americans who I consider successful as intellectual-activists, I did not perceive myself as being considered and outsider within my own community. In this case, not only was I of the same race and same class, but based on previous and subsequent discussions, I was perceived to be of the same cultural ideology.

IV
Participant Backgrounds

Introduction

This chapter is intended to enable the reader to "know," to the extent possible, the participants in this study. How the participants eventually define themselves will make sense as we uncover their respective backgrounds. The purpose of this chapter is to help the reader understand why each of the participants was chosen and to show the various bricks that compose the structure of the African-American intellectual-activist and the mortar that bonds each brick together.

First, I will describe the criteria for selection of participants. I have also included discussion on my relationship, if any, with each participant and how I came to select each individual. I have written about my initial impressions before each interview as well as my thoughts afterward. In some cases there will be information that comes from my observations of the participant in settings other than the formal interviews and the thoughts of others who know the participant.

Important to painting a picture of who each participant really is, is a description of his or her childhood, family structure, environment in which he or she was raised, college experiences and present career. I have also included information in the participants' own words that struck me as central to the understanding of their vantage points.

I have attempted to read between the lines of the narrated text to get at the essence of who each participant is. I discuss body language, attitude and responsiveness as I present brief biographies of the participants as individuals and my assessment of them as a group. In the next section I will discuss the criteria used to select the participants.

Criteria For Selection of Participants

Each of the participants was chosen because I classified him or her as an intellectual-activist. Therefore, there were two sets of criteria each participant had to satisfy: intellectual criteria and activist criteria.

I decided that holding a college degree should not automatically earn an individual the title of intellectual for the purposes of this study. In order for a person to meet the selection standards, he or she needed to demonstrate a serious interest in and pursuit of intellectual growth. There are several ways in which an individual can pursue intellectual growth.

One way to demonstrate an interest in intellectual stimulation is by holding a job that involves a constant building of one's body of academic, philosophical and scholarly knowledge. A college professorship is a good example of a job in which intellectual growth is nearly inevitable. Scholarly research is anywhere from encouraged to required depending on the level and type of institution with which one is affiliated.

Another acceptable demonstration of interest in intellectual growth is participation in structured college or university courses, either as a matriculated or non-matriculated student.

Yet another acceptable demonstration of interest in intellectual growth is participation in informal community settings such as book clubs or other discussion groups that foster intellectual stimulation. A serious independent education program, such as a personally motivated reading project or research work for the purpose of expanding one's knowledge base, can also demonstrate a commitment to intellectual growth.

Intellectualism, however, is only half the equation. Each participant also needed to satisfy the activist criteria. The requirement is active involvement in the improvement of the African-American community. There are several ways, for the purpose of this study, that I deemed acceptable for meeting the activist requirement.

One way to satisfy the activist criteria is through active membership in a community organization designed for the edification of the

African-American community. This membership can be unrelated to the participant's employment.

Another way to satisfy the activist requirement is employment at an African-American or non African-American institution designed for the improvement of the African-American community. The organizations to which I am referring are primarily grass roots community based organizations. However, an participant might work for a government or other non African-American owned institution which focusses their energies on the African-American community, such as the Boys and Girls Clubs, government social service agencies, colleges or universities located within the community.

It is also possible for an individual to meet the activist requirement through serious and committed activities in the community that are self-motivated and independent of any structured group.

I would like to make the point that although I have discussed the specific criteria for inclusion as an activist separately from the criteria for intellectuals, for these participants, the two aspects are almost inextricably linked to one another. Many of the participants, while satisfying the activist criteria, are also engaged in intellectual stimulation.

Each of the participants is between the ages of 45 and 65. Current events in one's community can have an effect on one's life. The aforementioned age range is small enough for some consistency, but large enough to allow for some variety. What follows is a description of the background of each of the participants. Pseudonyms are being used to protect the privacy of each participant.

Kwame Latif

I knew all along that Kwame would be one of my participants. After all, he was one of the people who inspired my research idea.

Kwame is a 45 year old university administrator and professor. He holds a doctorate in educational administration.

The interview took place in his office on the university campus. His office reflected the strong positive feelings he possessed of his

African-American heritage. The pictures on the wall represented African and African-American culture. The music played ranged from traditional jazz to contemporary rhythm and blues. His attire was reminiscent of the seventies, with dashikis and African jewelry.

Kwame was focussed and had obviously given a great deal of thought to this interview. He talked comfortably about his family situation and the deaths of his father and grandfather early in life. He described his father as having fallen, jumped or been pushed off of a bridge. His grandfather was the man of the house from the time he was six, when his father died, until he was 12, at which time his grandfather died.

He was very open about his teen and early college years in terms of the questionable activities in which he took part. He described his pre-college years in the work force and how his experiences in corporate America helped to shape his present life.

Kwame had always done well in school and it seemed that he had expectations for himself that went beyond a high school diploma. He gives credit to his mother for his discipline:

> I think that my mother did a tremendous job raising my sister and me. My mother didn't go past high school and my sister and I have six degrees between us and my sister is working on her Ph.D. She didn't irritate us in terms of pushing us but she always encouraged us. She insisted on a high level of discipline. And although I can't pinpoint what it was about my mother, she's largely responsible for my success and my sister's success.

Kwame believes that as African-Americans we have responsibilities. The first responsibility is that we have to study. If you are not a student, he still believes that you must study for the race. The second responsibility is to agitate the system wherever we are. The third responsibility is to rest as the first two responsibilities are very taxing.

Kwame became interested in a national grassroots organization while in college. His involvement with the group led him to start an independent school during the middle of his junior year. He was the director of this school, teacher at the school and all the while an undergraduate student at a midwestern college. The school was closed after four years when

Kwame started graduate work at a midwestern university. He continued at an ivy league institution in 1979 and he and his wife started another independent school there in 1980. His two sons attended the school until 1987 when the family left the west coast. He feels that the school kept him grounded amidst the credential driven ivy league university where he received his Ph.D. in Educational Administration in 1985.

So, from his scandal filled younger years to his administrative position at a major university, Kwame is truly a testament to the capacity for change. Kwame's leadership in the independent schools movement made him an ideal candidate for this research. He exemplifies commitment to African-American people through his social activism and his work, which blend well. Of his work, Kwame says:

> Virtually all of my research looks at African-American students because of my concern for that student population. Whether its looking at principals, looking at independent schools, looking at the enrollment and retention rate of African-American students in higher education. I see it all related to my primary concern which is the education, the success, the life chances of African-Americans.

Fatima Starks

Fatima is a 46 year old teacher. I had heard of Fatima through my work with a national grassroots organization. When I met her, she seemed very soft spoken and private. So I was pleasantly surprised at her openness throughout our interview. She told both the positive and the negative. Our relationship before the interview was a bit more developed than my relationships with most of the other participants. Although Spradley (1979) warns that this can be the source of some difficulty in the interviews, I felt that it worked well in this case. Spradley makes the point in his research that the more you know an participant outside of the participant/researcher relationship, and the closer you are to the community you have chosen to study, the more likely it is that the participant will make assumptions about your knowledge on the subject that is being discussed and give less detail than he or she would to a stranger not affiliated with the community. This was the case only to a small extent with Fatima. She realized that although we may have discussed an issue on another occasion, it was necessary for her to repeat certain things when asked and to go into more detail for the record.

Fatima wears salt and pepper dread locks and I can count the number of times that I have seen her without traditional African attire.

Fatima, like Kwame, grew up ina large northeastern city. I feel that this is an important point because growing up in a big city may suggest that one has at least had the opportunity to experience more and see more possibilities for success than a person who grew up during the same time period in a small townor rural area where exposure is somewhat limited.

She grew up in a housing project with both parents whom she describes as "uneducated" and five brothers and sisters. She attended a primarily white school as a result of the demands of the people in her community for better education for their children. She describes herself as a gifted child and veracious reader. Fatima had good, inspiring teachers who encouraged her academic achievement. Her mother did not accept failure and she was expected to do well in school, which she did all the way through high school.

She and her siblings attended a Presbyterian church in the neighborhood until she was about ten years old, at which time a Baptist church was built and they began attending it. Her parents did not go to church regularly, but insisted that the children did. Fatima stopped going once she became a teenager because of the contradictions and hypocrisy thatshe perceived within the church.

Although Fatima won a scholarship to go to college, she did not feel that she was emotionally ready to leaveher hometown. She was going through a great deal of upheaval with her family and moved in with her sister after high school. Like many other teenagers, Fatima rebelled through the use of hard drugs, including alcohol.

At the age of nineteen she became, in her words, "what some people would consider conscious." Her consciousness came about through her political readings and especially her re-reading of the *Autobiography of Malcolm X.* She says that she did not harbor an overabundance of anger towards whites and that her change was internal and very gradual. When she moved to the midwest, she had already decided to become a part of the African-American nationalist community. In the past she had been involved solely with African-American community organizations. Her move to Chicago was definitely a turning point for her.

I've had the opportunity to observe Fatima in other settings. She has made a commitment to the (African-American) Independent School movement. She worked with another independent school before her current position. Most of the participants who taught in independent schools in the seventies have taken more of an indirect role with them now as their careers have progressed and taken them to public schools, colleges and universities and entrepreneurial ventures. Her continued, direct involvement is what makes Fatima unique among this group of participants. She says of her involvement with the school:

> Some people were saying they were making lifetime commitments to the Shule. And I said I can't do that. I can look at myself every year. I intend to be here for a while. I could look at myself and what I'm doing and every year I have to rethink this commitment because I take it really seriously.

Gertrude Parker

Dr. Gertrude Parker, not unlike many of the participants, has southern roots, but grew up in a large midwestern city. She is a 62 year old college professor. She was open, honest and easy to interview. I explained the research to her, gave her loose guidance and the interview flowed.

She was openly critical of the African-American Nationalist community in her home town. Although she agreed with most, if not all of the African-American Nationalist tenets, she did not mince words when expressing the difficulty she had working with that community and what she perceived as their shortness on unity and abundance of hypocrisy. I sensed that having an opportunity to discuss her disenchantment was one of the reasons she was enthused about my request for an interview.

Dr. Parker has a Ph.D. in Educational Administration. This would be no surprise to the people who knew Gertrude when she was growing up.

She says that from very early people would tell her that she was a born leader and teacher. She received a great deal of encouragement from the African-American teachers at her elementary school.

In terms of family life, Gertrude was raised in a single parent home. She describes the economic state of her family as impoverished and her mother as a very strict disciplinarian. Dr. Parker identified with the African Methodist Episcopal (AME) church as she was growing up. During her high school years, she began, as she describes, developing a strong sense of autonomy. As a result, she pursued what many young girls thought was an escape hatch: marriage.

Subsequent to her marriage she had six children. Although times were difficult, criticism was abounding and support could have been better, she kept pushing and made a way out of what many might consider no way. She relied on her spirituality to motivate her success. Dr. Parker publishes a community newspaper in which issues of relevance and concern to the African-American community are addressed.

In discussing what motivates her activism and what she sees as the necessary element for positive change in the African-American community, Gertrude says:

> My source of strength is what I refer to is the grace of God, the most powerful. I have a very, very strong belief that we did not make ourselves and therefore, we have come from a Creator that is just and merciful and all this. That's one of the things that's missing. Spiritual development is missing. No matter what intellectual development you give to children, they must have spiritual development. And I'm not talking about just letting them go to the churches of their choice. They must be taught the values that were held by our ancestors and why those values were able to sustain them during the darkest period of their life which was the chattel slavery. We could not have survived that if our people did not have this deep and profound sense of connection to something greater than themselves. So our children don't get the spiritual development, which teaches them not just that Harriet Tubman did the Underground Railroad. That's good biography and that's good role modeling, but we must understand the reason why Harriet Tubman did that one time and continued to do that. We must understand who we were as a people, what the values were !

Dr. Parker has a beautiful aura. She is a very positive, but honest person. She has a very encouraging nature and claims her doctorate in the name of African-American people everywhere.

Denise Murphy

Denise is fifty seven years of age. She was born in the south and raised in the midwest. Denise is employed part time by the African-centered school her granddaughter attends.

Denise's voice is peaceful and strong at the same time. She seemed a bit nervous about our interview. It was very cathartic for her. At times, she seemed near the point of tears. I had only known Denise a few weeks before I knew that she would be a wonderful participant.

She talked almost exclusively about her father when I asked about the things in her upbringing that have contributed to the person she is today. She seemed to be heartbroken over the difficulty in her relationship with her dad. This heartbreak seems to have affected her entire life.

Denise grew up with her mother and sisters. Public aide was a fact of her life. She married young, divorced early and is unmarried to this day. Her only daughter and granddaughter live with her. She plays a large part in the upbringing of her granddaughter. Their relationship has been shaped by the experiences in Denise's life. Her activism comes in the form of her dedication to her granddaughter. She is determined to make sure she grows up to be a strong African-American woman.

Her interview was an emotional one. I sensed that she is still harboring the pain from the loss of her ex-husband from divorce and finally her father from death. She has taken that pain and become a stronger person both because of and in spite of it. Her interview outlined the stages of her growth.

> I was a dad's girl. I loved my dad. In fact, just thinking about him and talking about the fact that I was born, I haven't really thought about him in a little while. He's been dead now about thirteen years. And I loved

> him so much for so long. And I hurt so much because he left us when I was about ten years old and it just changed my life around.

In retrospect, she attributes his desertion to the pressures of being a African-American man in America.

Denise describes feelings of having always wanted more. She gives a great deal of credit to her two grandmothers. She states:

> I'd never heard of fish gravy but my mother said that my grandmother kept her head high. When they had one fish divided between eight of them, watered down with gravy. And no one had ever heard of fish gravy until my dad's mother.

This is Denise' testament to the strength and pride of the African-American women in her life. The breakup of her marriage was one of the stressful situations that forced her to fall back on the traditional strength of the women in her family and I sensed from our discussion that she draws often on this ancestral strength.

> Because we were given life we are, it's just important that we leave this earth a better place. You have to make corrections where you see wrongs. We owe it to our ancestors, not only in a general sense, but to our specific ancestors. I was taught truth. I hope to start raising consciousness through my own daughter and granddaughter. Our family line hinges upon if I do for my granddaughter what my grandmother did for me. If I can do just a portion of that, than my life here on earth has been worthwhile.

Hasani Moyo

My interview with Hasani really began the moment I finally reached him long distance by phone. I was told by a good friend that he would probably be willing to participate in my research and would give an interesting interview.

Hasani is a 52 year old college professor and business owner. Books played a major role in developing his consciousness and he has chosen to offer the gift of literature to the African-American community through his business and his teaching.

When I finally reached him, which took about three calls, I told him by whom I was referred, what my research was about and finally asked if I would be able to interview him. He said something to the effect of " . . . don't ask if you can interview me, lots of people want to interview me. If what you want is help with you dissertation, I'd be glad to do that."

Quite frankly, I found his comments somewhat intimidating. But, I appreciated his honesty and willingness to be interviewed. I traveled over five hundred miles to make this happen.

The interview was at his business office. The building was humble but impressive. He seemed very prepared for the interview. I didn't have to do very much talking. I led him with a few guiding questions and he took off from there.

He spoke very candidly of his unstable home life as a child with a junkie mother and no father to be seen. The interview was powerful. He seems to take his past in stride. In fact, he practically credits his past experiences hustling with his current entrepreneurial success.

Hasani is married, with three children. He was one of the two male participants who spoke of his wife and her strength without having to be asked specifically.

One of the outstanding themes in Hasani's upbringing was his life without a father and a mother who died young as a result of drug addiction. He talks about his mother's problems very matter-of-factly and doesn't seem the least bit bitter. Hasani was on his own very early in life. After the death of his mother, he moved to the midwest with nothing and did what it took to survive. He credits his mother with introducing him to a book by Richard Wright at the age of 13 that "put me on the road to the life that I'm in today." This book was the beginning of his discovery of African-American literature and the power of ideas. This love of this power kept him from a great deal of the trouble that a boy alone and poor in a big city could have gotten into.

The other experience that stood out as crucial in his interview was his experience in the military service. He ended up in the United States Army at the age of 17. He says that by this time he had begun to put himself on a reeducation program. During basic training he personally experienced the racism that exists in the military. He was challenged by a drill sergeant regarding the book he was reading at the time.

> I started reading rather deeply in Black literature and on the way to basic training I had a book and when I got off the bus the drill sergeant saw Paul Robeson's face on the book and snatched the book from my hand and said "what's yo' Negro mind doing reading this Black communist." So he told all the recruits to line up against the bus and he took the book and held it with his hand and tore the pages out and gave the pages to each recruit and told them to use it for toilet paper. And of course, several thoughts went through my mind. What am I doing here, number one. And two, here I'm putting myself in a position in the authority of men less intelligent than I am who are gonna be giving me orders. But the third thing was that this is a book and this book frightened this man so much and of course it was the content of the book, then there must really be something important about ideas.

He began at this point, to think about his life with much more clarity, as he describes it. Of course, after his three years were over, he did not reenlist. Immediately after his discharge he began working for the African-American struggle. Much of Hasani's consciousness seems to have come from reading. This concept of the power of ideas was central to this interview and to his life.

Of the solutions to the challenges being faced by African-Americans today, Hasani says:

> I think that we have to really, because there is a real schism in our community, but we have to realize that we cannot short change the intellectual development of any of our people, girls or boys, women or men. And if we are to really have any effect, make any effect in this struggle, we need more and more men and women who are intelligent, i.e. intellectuals, but intellectuals with a small "i" and workers with a large "w." You see, cultural workers, that people realize that even if you

> have to work eight, nine hours for somebody else, then it seems to me that you need to be givin' at least ten, eleven hours to your own community somehow. And that may be in making sure that your own children don't end up crazy. The mothers and fathers may not get any pat on the back, but the point is that they made a great contribution because you and your brothers and sisters are not out there sticking people up and having goo gobs of babies and not taking care of them. I mean, these are the small things, but the small things end up being the very large things, you see, in the final analysis.

Barbara Gray

Ms. Gray is 58 years of age and was born and raised inthe midwest. She is a teacher in an African-centered school. Ms. Gray is actively involved in an organization that studies ancient Egyptian culture or Kemetic culture.

Barbara describes her early childhood as having been spent around people who were involved in the arts, especially music. Her grandmother was able to open a business in the downtown area. Much of her family was college educated. She talked about being encouraged to go into teaching so that she and her children would have the same hours and summers off. The family spent summers in the country on a farm they owned in Michigan. "But I look back on it now and think how fortunate we were because I could never afford two houses for **my** children."

Barbara attended a large university on the west coast immediately after high school. She did pursue teaching and taught for thirty four years in a public school system. Those years brought both positive and negative experiences. She is currently teaching on the elementary level at an African-centered school.

In Barbara's classroom, one can have each of the senses stimulated. The sweet smell of incense is always in the air. African fabric covers the windows and desks. Each sixth grade child has a hand made pillow in the room.

Barbara calls herself an African, not Black, not Afro-American, not African-American, simply and completely African. She states:

> You know, if you ask someone from Poland what are they, they say Polish. If you ask someone from China what are they, they say

> Chinese." She goes on to say that more strength comes from the implications of being African. "I mean, you're coming from the first civilization !

Barbara, however, is not among the participants who has taken an African name.

I would say that Barbara comes from a different economic class than most of the other participants. Many came from single parent homes, all from homes where money was in short supply. Many experienced a life supported by Public Aid. In several cases, this struggle contributed, at least in part, to the strength of character they possess today. This past struggle seems to motivate their dedication. Barbara is as dedicated as any of the other participants, her foundation, her source, is simply different. This will be an important part of the analysis. It is not necessary for a community to come from the same place or even take the same route to progress. The final goal is what unifies. And that goal is the uplift of people of African descent, however one defines that. Ani (1994) might disagree. She writes that what makes progress valid is that most people agree that it is progress. I define progress as movement toward the ideal. If an individual is moving toward his or her concept of ideal, he or she, in my mind, has made valid progress. This progress is valid whether or not I agree with their perception of ideal.

Barbara summarizes the purpose of her activism this way:

> When cultures with contradictory versions of reality collide, children are often the casualties of that contact. I summons Sankofa (our ancestor wisdom) to increase our consciousness of who we are and what we are about. Thereby, I hope to create conditions for an inventory of the wonderful warehouse that is our past thus providing a vehicle for safe conduct into our futures.

Karimah Salaam

Karimah is 47 years old and was born on the east coast. She is an entrepreneur with her own consulting firm.

I sensed that Karimah was holding back in the interview. She often mentioned some pain and dysfunction in her upbringing and current life. When asked to explain, she avoided direct answers. In subsequent discussions, she explained that she is a very private person. Even so, she made a valuable contribution to this research.

She was separated from her parents very early and was raised by Seventh Day Adventist foster parents. She feels that their religion and basic philosophy of life gave her a strong spiritual foundation. She describes her foster parents as "primarily vegetarian people who lived a life free of television."

She was reunited with her mother at the age of eight at which time she, her brother and mother moved to a large midwestern city.

She attended a multicultural elementary school where she had positive experiences with teachers both African-American and White and became involved in the African-American cultural movement under the leadership of a teacher who was one of the founders of the Student National Coordinating Committee (SNCC).

Karimah credits her African-American consciousness to her teachers, as her mother worked quite a bit. She describes her mother as an avid reader who did not have time to sit down and teach her children. However, she believes that she and her brother were well loved and cared for.

Karimah became more deeply involved in the movement during her first year of college. She attended a teachers college in the midwest and was married after her first year. She had intended to be a teacher because of the positive impact her teachers had upon her life.

An important issue that was raised by Karimah was that of skin color. She says that her family was very color conscious and she was the darkest.

> So it was always a thing of what beauty is and what beauty isn't. And when the movement came along and Black became beautiful it was almost like I had stepped out of a cocoon.

Today Karimah is very comfortable with who she is both physically and spiritually. She is one of the six participants who uses and African name and one of only three who has had her name changed legally.

Her self confidence and self comfort were the things that made me believe she would be an interesting participant. For many years, she was a part of an established African-American sisterhood group and received a great deal of strength and support through it.

In response to a question about the goals of her activism Karimah says:

> I've seen bits and pieces of it everywhere. And that gives me hope. And when I see that we're still having children, that gives me hope. It also gives me a responsibility because the idea is to be and know who you are and act out of that. That's the ideal. I am now going into elderhood and so that I become a role model or a teacher or whatever. I don't want to say a whatever. A person who could provide guidance to others who are coming along the way so that they may not make some of the same errors or they may get some information earlier because they can handle it earlier than when I got it.

John Drew

John Drew is a 58 year old former public school teacher and administrator. I met John at a conference sponsored by the Chicago Teachers Union. The topic of my dissertation came up in conversation. When John's colleagues heard that I was interested in studying African-American Nationalists, they became excited and suggested that I interview John. He seemed interested so we talked a bit. He gave me his card and a few weeks later I scheduled the interview.

John Drew is a recently retired public school teacher and administrator. He seemed very enthusiastic about the interview. I opened his interview as I had opened all others before his by asking what in his upbringing has contributed most to the person he is today.

He began by talking about his activities as a student at a New Jersey high school. Although he had the ability, he says that he was not a "great" student. He played varsity football and baseball. Football would take him to an historically African-American University in the southeast. He describes his experience at this school as a wonderful one filled with nurturing teachers sincerely interested in their students.

He first began playing leadership roles with a boy scout troop at his church. Immediately after college, he was drafted into the Army. John describes his military experience as bittersweet. He enjoyed the competition, not necessarily against others, but with himself, "to see how you stacked up in a disciplined environment," as he put it. In 1959 when he was first drafted, he encountered racism. But all in all, he believes that he did a great deal of growing up because of this experience.

John came to themidwest through his placement with the military. He made the decision to teach in the area. This was the point in his life where he began to find himself. He began to realize that people listened to him and that he was able to influence people. He targeted his activities toward youngsters. John was in the classroom for nine years them moved to instructional television then to administration until his recent retirement.

When asked to define himself with regard to African-American nationalism he says that he does not consider himself a nationalist. He's not been affiliated with African-American nationalist groups but he says "I do understand and lean toward and have empathy for and often support many of the things that they say."

He believes strongly that there should be an African-American agenda. When asked which things he would put on his personal African-American agenda, he speaks in detail about economic independence through entrepreneurship. He feels that the African-American church can be the conduit to this independence. He is actively involved in trying to make things happen.

> My retirement is not one. I didn't take it so that I could go and sit on the sidelines and just kind of cop out. I took it because I realized that I had done just about as much as I could do with the institutions that I worked for. But I see myself in a position now of being able to provide service, and in some instances to the school system, where I can negotiate directly with the school or with the community to be able to serve as a resource.

John stands out as the only participant who is convinced that the solutions to many of the problems in the African-American community can and should come through the church. He did not present himself as a religious man, simply one who believes in the strength and potential of the African-American church. In discussing African-American nationalism and what is necessary for the African-American community John says:

> I think the most important thing that should supersede any movement is who you are and what your true nature is. Then I think you have to make your choices based on that and shouldn't be made exclusively on any groups tenets because then you become a puppet or a pawn. But there should be an African-American agenda, or a Black agenda, most definitely. And I'm certainly for organizations and individuals of different persuasions who are African-American to come together and hammer out a common agenda for that. But to say that they all have to walk block step down the street together, no.

Hakim Asante

I interviewed Hakim at my home. He seemed very comfortable. He is 59 years old and was raisedon the east coast. Hakim recently retired as a public school teacher and is currently an independent educational consultant.

Hakim grew up with both parents who he described as very strong in their racial beliefs. He had a good undergraduate experience at an historically Black university where he was "totally immersed in Blackness."

Hakim is another one of the participants who joined the United States military. He did so, as many of the others did, because financially, it seemed the only way to get by. Hakim's goal was to become a doctor and the military would provide the money necessary to achieve this goal.

Along the way, Hakim ended up teaching school inthe midwest. He began to see how bad things were and decided to go into teaching believing that he had something to contribute to the children and the community.

The public school system in which he taught was, in his words, "overtly racist without pretense," at that time. It was difficult for African-American teachers to become certified. Hakim stayed with it and now thirty years later, he has just retired from the same high school at which he began teaching in the early sixties.

Unlike other participants who were turned off by and never returned to the racist military, Hakim enjoyed the challenge and used it to the advantage of African-American people.

The main themes pulled from our discussion were his love and concern for African-American students now and during his tenure with the public school system and his commitment to African-American nationalist tenets. Hakim was one of the few participants who welcomed the African-American nationalist label.

He is currently a consultant specializing in African-centered education and regularly writes articles on the subject for a variety of journals and newspapers. His concern for the fate of the African-American community can be summarized in one line. Of the struggle of people of African descent in this country to gain freedom he says "this is war !"

Malome Sule

Malome is a 45 year old university professor. He was born in a small town in the midwest. He was raised by his grandparents in a segregated setting.

He became aware of himself as an African-American early on. During his early elementary school years, he was in a segregated school. His teachers taught their students to be proud of being "Negro." This was a safe and comfortable environment. He moved to an integrated setting shortly after the beginning of his elementary education. It was there that he became aware of the negative connotations attached to being of African descent in this country.

Malome grew beyond the negativity and went on to high school and college where he became actively engaged in learning more about the history of the African-American experience. He says:

> There was a guy from Chicago and he was the one who really started talking to me about pride in the race and consciousness of it. He gave me a carved wooden head called a teke head, and everybody was wearing those in those days. It was like a symbol of pride. And I was wearing mine because now I was becoming aware of myself where I had been ignorant all this time. And I wanted everything I could get in terms of knowledge. And so I was reading whatever I could get my hands on and outwardly attempting to show this pride.

This thirst for knowledge and further cultural development continued in Malome. In the seventies, he became involved in a nationalist organization that would shape the course of his life.

He was one of the founders of an independent school in the northeast where he was completing his doctorate and went on to open another independent school in the early nineties. He is currently a professor at a major research institution where research is expected and required of the faculty. His research focusses primarily on issues relating to African-American people. He has dedicated a significant portion of his time to mentoring African-American students.

Malome was part of my pilot study seven years ago. He was selected as an intellectual-activist because of his commitment to African-American people through his official (as a professor) and unofficial (as an individual) acts that have fostered the development of cultural growth in a significant number of people.

Oba Poole

I met Oba through my work at an African-American nationalist organization in Chicago. He is soft spoken but opinionated. This is how I became interested in him as in participant. Sixty something Oba is a social worker by training and a community activist and educational consultant.

Oba came from a poor family who depended on the government for financial support. He was raised with two brothers and both parents. He had a tremendous amount of support from his extended family.

When asked to describe his upbringing and his family, he emphasized that fact that he had a wonderfully happy childhood and simply adored his father. He described his dad as an extraordinary man who was a well respected artist and a communist. He credits his activism to the example set by his father.

Oba's own personal activism began in high school where he wrote political essays and began to express concerns about social conditions for African-Americans. According to Oba, his female school teachers also had a profound effect on his development. They encouraged his writing.

After high school he went to a predominantly white junior college and was not very involved with the campus community. He did continue to write independently. He decided to go into social work because all of the people that he admired were in helping professions.

Oba says that he never had a sense that he would be anchored in poverty. Because of the visions of his family, he had no doubt that he would go far in life.

> Well, the family and most families have had visions of motivating to be better and you expect them to. So, it was automatic. In fact, the idea of doing poorly at school was an embarrassment, contrary to what you hear today. We were very competitive in school, we wanted to do well, we strived and worked hard to do well in school. So this is true in most of the families. There haven't been poor families that haven't worked hard. Education is important.

Currently, Oba is a poet, playwright and social activist. His works have been widely published. He also plays an active role on the Board of Directors for an African-centered school.

Summary

All but one of the participants had a strong family support system during their respective upbringings. Many came from strong two parent households. Most of those who came from single parent households had extended family at the ready.

Each of the participants could be categorized as an "educator." This term is being used in a restricted sense and refers to a person who teaches in a school, college or university setting.

Further, each of the participants could be considered part of the "African-American Middle Class." This class has been defined in many ways, most commonly based on the kind of job one holds or the amount of money one makes. A unionized blue collar worker who sweeps floors at a factory may very well make more money than a teacher but generally the teacher is considered a part of the African-American middle class where the sweeper is not (see Edwards and Spurlock, 1988, Kronus, 1971).

The point, however, is that this group of African-Americans has a socioeconomic status that many do not. Yet they have not chosen to simply wallow in their success. They have chosen not simply to give back, but to dedicate their lives to the uplift of people of African descent. Some of the participants concentrate their efforts on African-Americans. Those who consider themselves Pan-Africanists feel a connection to all people of African descent both on the continent and in the diaspora. Either way, all are working toward making a positive change for African-American people.

What makes these participants special and similar is that they have committed themselves to the service of the African-American masses. In the next chapter, I will discuss the common factor among them, a positive African-American self concept.

Profile of Participants

Pseudonym	Age	Gender	Occupation	Highest Educ.	Birth-place
Kwame Latif	45	Male	Professor	Doctorate	Northeast
Fatima Starks	46	Female	Teacher	Associate	Northeast
Gertrude Parker	62	Female	Professor	Doctorate	South
Denise Murphy	57	Female	Office Manager	Masters	South
Hasani Moyo	52	Male	Professor/ Business Owner	Masters	Midwest
Barbara Gray	58	Female	Teacher	Masters	Midwest
Karimah Salaam	47	Female	Business Owner	Bachelors	Midwest
John Drew	58	Male	Retired School Administrator	Masters	Northeast
Hakim Asante	59	Male	Retired Teacher	Masters	New England
Malome Sule	45	Male	Professor	Doctorate	Midwest
Oba Poole	61	Male	Social Worker/Writer	Masters	Midwest

V

The Development of a Positive African-American Self Concept

Introduction

The overall theme that emerged from the data was that of positive African-American self concept. Gordon (1976) wrote:

> The history of Blacks in America is a record of the mergence of an oppressed people from conditions of slavery as a moral-legal order to conditions of existence as a group of low caste and class within the society. It is against this background that the generalized Negro personality, the Black youth's racial awareness and the self concept of Black Americans is presumed to have developed into negative self evaluations. (pg.373)

Gordon takes a quantitative approach to challenge the generalization that African-Americans possess low self concept. She found that "patterns of conflicting findings make generalized statements about low Black self concept questionable." My qualitative approach using the life history method reveals that in the case of at least 11 African-Americans, a positive self concept is not out of the ordinary. My findings demonstrate that positive personal experiences can outweigh negative social historical experiences in the development of self concept. What follows will be a discussion of the experiences of the participants in this study. Their experiences have been categorized under several themes. The themes are:

African-American self concept defined in terms of African-American nationalism and Afrocentricity, African-American self concept as defined in terms of religion, African-American self concept as defined in terms of family and African-American self concept defined in terms of formal schooling experiences. I will discuss each of these themes as part of a topic I have labeled the development of a positive African-American self concept.

I will use the theory of symbolic interactionism to interpret the theme of African-American self concept that has emerged from my data. Further, I will discuss the idea of self concept as it is described in the literature and theories of self concept that address issues specific to African-Americans. I will tie together the principles of symbolic interactionism and the issues that contribute to the development of self concept for African-American people. Finally, I will discuss the relationship between self concept and the life purposes of the participants involved in this study within the framework of the "struggle for significance" as developed by Brennecke and Amick (1975) and the concept of "the Black self" as described by Wyne (1974). In the next section, I will talk about a specific kind of activism, African-American nationalism, and the role it has played and is playing in the lives of the participants in this study.

African-American Self Concept Defined in Terms of African-American Nationalism and Afrocentricity

Background

With an increased orientation toward Black significant others as the basis for self evaluation, Black consciousness has great potential for helping Blacks attain self realization and for helping them to overcome the strong negative self imagery emanating from reflections in a white mirror. (Wyne, 1974, pg. 88)

In this section, I will discuss the feelings of the participants with regard to African-American nationalism and Afrocentricity. All of those interviewed have a direct relationship with the African-American nationalist community. I found as I proceeded with this research that often African-centered and Afrocentric are used synonymously with African-American nationalism by people within the community. In a 1970 book edited by Bracey, Meier and Rudwick, the term African-American nationalism has been used in American history to describe a body of social thought, attitudes and actions ranging from the simplest expressions of ethnocentrism and racial solidarity to comprehensive and sophisticated ideologies of Pan-Negroism or Pan-Africanism. They define Black cultural nationalism as the belief that:

> Black people in the United States or throughout the world have a culture, style of life, cosmology, approach to the problems of existence and aesthetic values distinct from that of white Americans in particular and white Europeans or westerners in general. (pg. xxvi)

Afrocentric, as defined by Molefi Asante (1988), is an advanced level of consciousness that is reached after several stages of a complex transformation. I've found, through lengthy discussions with the participants, that only four of them welcome the tenets **and** title of African-American nationalist, although all were in agreement with some portion of African-centeredness. All but one of the participants have direct involvement with an African-centered institution; four were directly responsible for starting African-centered schools. Seven either sit on the Board of Directors of, teach at or have their child(ren) enrolled in an African-centered school. Most participants have presented seminars on African-centered education.

So, the affiliations with African-centeredness and African-American nationalism are strong. However, when describing themselves specifically, less than half wanted to be considered African-American nationalists.

Many define themselves by way of physical manifestations. The three main categories used for definition within the present participant group are hair, attire and names. In this group, many statements were being made without words. Each of the participants wears his or her hair in its natural state. Ten of the eleven participants have a considerable wardrobe of African attire. (The eleventh may, but I do not spend enough time around him to make that observation.) Six of the participants use a name of African origin.

Akoto (1992) writes that:

> To deny the cultural, spiritual, psychological consequences of that (African-American) history is lunacy. To consciously affirm that cultural dynamic in thought and behavior and then institutionalize that dynamic is Afrocentric.

Akoto begins the chapter on Afrocentricity in his book on nationbuilding with a discussion of cultural nationalism in other countries in Europe and Asia and how it was seen as acceptable and even necessary, in some cases, to the survival of that particular culture. He writes further that when the nationalist movement surfaced among Africans in America, it was seen as possessing "no intrinsic value" (pg. 72)

Akoto eloquently states that:

> Several studies, common sense and the twenty odd years of the independent school movement have demonstrated conclusively that cognitive development as well as social and emotional maturation, is most effectively achieved when the cultural context, the academic content and the physical environment is aligned and consistent with the cultural orientation of the child.

Afrocentricity is the new buzzword. In my observation, many people (of African and European descent) seem to feel more comfortable with the term Afrocentric than with African-American nationalist. It seems that nationalism has more political, revolutionary implications. Many African-American Baptist churches are now calling themselves Afrocentric, but I've never heard of them being referred to as nationalist. Nationalism is generally associated with the sixties and radicalism. The **word** Afrocentric even seems to sound less threatening. Yet from the writings of experts in the field (see for example Akoto, 1992, Asante, 1988, Madhubuti, 1973), Afrocentric, African-centered and African-American nationalism are terms that are interchangeable.

Most of the participants, although acknowledging a belief in Afrocentric, nationalist tenets, refuse the African-American nationalist title. This debate is similar to the even more fundamental one of what we, as people of African descent in America, should call ourselves. The current acceptable choices appear to be Black, Afro-American, African-American or African. In a 1994 speech by Gwendolyn Brooks at Chicago State University, this debate was addressed.

Dr. Brooks stated that she prefers BLACK !, as it has more political implications. She spoke about the concept that this term encompasses all people of African descent as opposed to African-American which excludes continental Africans, West Indians and Blacks who live in Canada and Europe. She jokingly talks about how African-American sort of rolls off the tongue in a non-threatening, sing-songy sort of way.

The participants involved in this study were chosen because they were either self-proclaimed African-American nationalists or so closely affiliated with the African-American nationalist community that it is generally assumed by members within and outside of the community that they are nationalists. This issue of self-definition was raised in each interview and surprisingly, many of the participants did not feel comfortable with the African-American nationalist label. The participants who felt this way did not see the rejection of this label as compromising their African-American self concept. The reason they felt uncomfortable with the title was based, for the most part, on issues of sincerity within the nationalist community.

Participant Feelings About the Nationalist Label

The most popular reason for discomfort with the African-American nationalist label was some form of disappointment with the African-American nationalist community. Several participants talked about negative experiences preventing them from adopting the label. Most expressed believing in the goals of the African-American nationalist community but having some problems with the lip service that was being given to certain values associated with nationalism without the follow-through. Gertrude says:

> Nationalists have disappointed me also because they don't support the things they claim to really desire. They talk about liberation, they talk Nguzo Saba, the Black value system, but they don't build the institutions, they don't support the institutions . . . the people called it whatever they felt like calling it and they said it's nationalist to educate your children at home, it's nationalist to ah, change your name, you know, but its not nationalist to believe in reciprocity, to believe that those things from which you extract some benefit are deserving of your support. Consequently we see this kind of situation where you have in Chicago that has what, a million and a half Black people that you have one school, one independent school. Cause the nationalists have their children every place you can find Black children. They have their children in the public schools they have them in the Catholic schools, they have them in the private schools . . . So by wondering, well what is the point of Nationalism. Is it meaning after all of your sacrifices, after all of your vegetarianism and your wearing your cultural dress and your changing your name and your Nguzo Saba and your house with all the pictures of Black things on the wall; if you are still throwing up your confetti when your child gains entrance into a white institution, you know, if you're still throwing up confetti when you find enough financial aid to be able to send your child to a private college, which is definitely trying to make sure that those children get into the mainstream of America, are you serious?!

This kind of disappointment surfaces in several interviews. Karimah says, on the question of identification with the African-American nationalist label:

> No. I identify myself as an African-American woman. And I am interested in promoting, helping, assisting in whatever would push us forward. I at one time would have probably identified myself as a Black nationalist. But I'm not sure what that means now because there was enough history behind it to say to me that's something I have to explore further before saying that's what I am.

When asked about her affiliation with a nationalist organization she responded:

> I had no problems fitting in because (the organization's) goals are my goals. I'm not into labels anymore. I think labels get you in trouble because what I find is that people in the community who call themselves nationalists do things that I would never do. And there are other people in the community who probably wouldn't do some of the things I did. But primarily I believe in honesty, in trust, commitment and not the commitment that comes out of a bunch of words but the commitment that comes out of your actions. And I need to see it and over the years I have seen things that have made me feel like, no, I am not a Black nationalist.

Kujichagulia (self determination), is one of the Nguzo Saba (seven principles of Blackness). It says that as African-Americans we should "define ourselves, name ourselves, create for ourselves and speak for ourselves rather than being defined, named, created and spoken for by others" (Karenga, 1988). Karimah and Gertrude demonstrate how this principle can be used not only in relation to the larger society, but within the community as well. Although I don't believe that one must be a nationalist to affect change in a positive way in the African-American community, I was surprised at the number of participants I assumed would identify themselves as nationalists who did not.

Hakim is certainly an example of an participant who takes pride in the nationalist label. Below, he speaks of his commitment to cultural nationalism:

> . . . We started our own school, a revolutionary school to train community kids to be warriors for our struggle. We were revolutionary and that was an extension of our ideology, was to organize and build institutions. We were cultural nationalists. We were advocates of the Nguzo Saba. We chose to follow Maulana Karenga's and (name inaudible's) cultural nationalist strategy as pertaining to the Panther ideology and some of the other ideologies that were in the community and that got me started in the independent school movement.

Fatima spoke of her nationalism throughout her interview and in previous and subsequent conversations. She considers herself a nationalist teacher and is very concerned about what it means to be a nationalist teacher. She describes her development into a nationalist as an evolution of sorts.

> It wasn't like . . . it was just a slow change. It wasn't like a blinding light. I just, the more I read, I just started putting things together internally. I just started developing this nationalist, I guess I could say, theory.

She has made innumerable personal sacrifices in the name of nationalism but does not regret the way and extent to which she has chosen to commit herself to African-American people by serving as a nationalist teacher.

> And you were used, but I knew and I understood. I think I went through alot of things that I went through because I understood why I was there and I understood what my commitment was. And I just kind of went around the foolishness and the ignorance and the backwardness for the sake of the children.

Oba and Barbara straddled the fence on the nationalist label question. Each agreed that they were nationalists but just didn't use the label often but did not object to the label. Oba states:

> Well right now I think I'm still a nationalist because of my total commitment to the Black community. Pan Africanist is much broader by my extension to the African diaspora. So I feel comfortable but these labels are so relative. There's good nationalism and bad nationalism. There's so many forms of nationalism. It's not a word I use to describe myself, basically I'm committed to Black people and helping to deal with all these problems and I assume that falls under the umbrella of nationalism. But I feel comfortable with that.

Afrocentric Appearance

Each of the participants is African-centered in his/her physical appearance; this includes hairstyle and adornments, i.e. jewelry and clothing. Although names are not necessarily a physical representation, they will also be included in this discussion on symbols of African-centeredness. Based on participant interviews, these physical representations of African-centeredness are very important parts of their lives.

Karimah, who usually dresses in African-centered attire talks about why she wears Eurocentric corporate attire at certain times:

> If external factors will keep me from getting done what needs to be done, so be it. The question to myself is am I trying to make a statement or get a job. Who I am will come through regardless of what I am wearing.

Karimah goes on to say that if she were asked to straighten her hair, she would refuse. She believes that external things such as clothing are simply an **expression** of who she is, not the essence of who she is. She sees her hair, however, as a more fundamental part of her and insists on wearing it in its natural state.

There are two symbols being used in this example: clothing and hair. In the above example with participant Karimah, she has first made the decision that her hair and her attire are symbols of her Blackness. Further, she has come to somewhat different conclusions with regard to each of these symbols that represent her Blackness. The decision had been made by Karimah long before any particular situation occurred, that the wearing of her hair in its natural state was not something to be negotiated. She further decided that clothing is a symbol of her Blackness that she is willing to alter if she believes it is necessary after analyzing a particular situation. The difference, as she explains it, is that "when I came out (of the womb) this is how my hair was and this is how it will stay." She sees her clothing as an expression of her Blackness but not part of the essence of her Blackness.

The basic principles of symbolic interactionism as developed by Mead (1934) and further expanded by Brumer (1969) suggest that human beings are endowed with the capacity for thought that is shaped by social interaction where they learn the meanings and symbols that allow them to exercise this capacity for thought. Symbols are important in this portion of my analysis as they contribute to the development of the positive African-American self concept of the participants in this study. Meanings and symbols, which for the current study can include such things as hairstyle, attire, names and culturally based phrases, allow people to carry on action and interaction. The theory further implies that people are able to modify or alter the meanings and symbols they use in action and interaction based on their interpretation of a situation.

An example relevant to the current study is that most of the participants wear African attire, but when they need to interact with a community in which they believe cultural attire will send a message that will not be respected or understood in the way that it is intended, they will wear traditional American corporate attire. This is in keeping with yet another principle of symbolic interactionism which says that people are able to make modifications and alterations in the symbols and meanings they use because, in part, of their ability to interact with themselves, which allows them to examine possible courses of action, assess their relative advantages and disadvantages and choose a course of action.

Fatima talks about the importance of her hair in expressing her African-Americanness:

> Well in 1968 I stopped straightening it. I started out with a, I call it a set natural, when you set your hair wet with rollers and pick it out. And so really since '68 I haven't straightened it. I went from there to in the '70's I started braiding and I'd go from braids to natural. In the '80's I started thinking about dread locks, late '80's. I thought about it for five years when I was going from braids. I went from braids to twists and then I started saying I need to stop putting other people's hair inside of my head. So I stopped the braids and started twisting and put a —— in your hair for that. And then I decided I needed to stop putting everything else in my hair and just go ahead on and lock up. So I started that in '92 and finally in July they all locked up.

As is evident from the 25 year transformation, it was not an easy decision for Fatima to 'lock' her hair. Locking is a natural style worn by many men and women of African descent. The decision is difficult because when the hair locks it is nearly impossible to comb it out. Therefore the decision to lock is relatively permanent. If an individual changes his or her mind, the most common method is to cut the locks off and start over. In the African-American community it is often said that a woman's hair is her crowning glory. Madame C.J. Walker, the first self made female millionaire in this country, made her millions by marketing methods for African-American women to straighten their hair. Dread locks are not accepted to the extent that straightened hair is. An African-American woman who wears her hair in its natural state, especially when that state is kinky, is still questioned in the 1990's. Presumably the root of this non-acceptance of natural Blackness by African-Americans is some level of self hatred. Conversely, flaunting Blackness can be viewed as a certain level of self acceptance. Wyne speaks to this phenomenon.

> The shift away from attempts to mask Blackness with skin bleaches and hair straighteners towards attempts to express, even flaunt, Blackness represents much more than a superficial and cosmetic appearance. It represents a major change in the fiber from which the new Black self is woven. (Wyne, 1974, pg. 87)

The Black self as defined by Wyne will be discussed in more depth following a more fundamental discussion on the importance of self definition for African-Americans, which will be placed within the context of Brennecke's and Amick's (1975) work on selfhood and the struggle for significance.

African Names

Six of the participants use African names. None of the participants were given African names at birth. Therefore, each made a conscious decision to use a name of African origin as a first, middle and/or last name.

The degree to which African names were used varied. Some participants have had their names legally changed, some use the African name in all settings, but have not changed it legally. Some use their African names in cultural settings, but use their birth names at other times. Kwame, who legally changed his name more than twenty years ago, relays an experience he had with his sister that tells of his feelings about names:

> When we had the naming ceremony, we have naming ceremonies for our children, for my second child, my sister sat through it crying, which is not unusual because my sister is very emotional. But she told me that the reason she was crying was that she realized that our name, Long, was not going to be carried on after our generation because the children did not have the name Long. So that was an emotional moment for her because it was the end of the family tree, so to speak. Which to me, and I didn't say this to her then but, that's totally ridiculous because the children are going to live and they're going to have children. I mean, what's the significance of the name, which is somebody else's name anyway. I think it's more significant to have the Latif name carried on.

Hasani also had his name legally changed more than twenty years ago.

> So when I come to the table, I'm coming to the table with the same kind of power or resources as those with who you're trying to negotiate with, number one, also that's why I changed my name. You walk into the room as Hasani Moyo, that's alot different than walking into the room as David Jones. You see what I'm saying. Because it took a certain consciousness to move toward the identifying with one's culture, you see. Especially with a name as difficult as mine . . . and, but you do that because you're trying to essentially do what all people do who are in control of their own cultural imperatives, that is that they're washed in their own culture, therefore they become very secure. And so as a secure Black man who have no doubts about who he is, than I can go any place in the world and I'm gon' function, you see, at the same level of the people I gotta deal with, you see, because I don't have any doubts. I'm not gon' ever apologize for being who I am.

Karimah decided to change her name long before she actually changed it. In the name of west African tradition, she did not want to choose her own name, she wanted to be named by an elder. Of her experience she says:

> People were changing their names very frequently in the early, late sixties, early seventies. I wanted to change my name because I felt, Cassie was my name, which is Greek and I wasn't identifying with the Greeks. But I didn't want to change my name because of a name that I just picked out of a book because I liked it. And so I have a friend whose a griot from west Africa and when he first came in 1977, I asked him if he would pick and choose the time that he would name me. So in 1983 is when he named me. I wanted him to . . . I wanted somebody to observe me and tell me how they saw my behaviors and my person because I think, or at least for me that was closer to me being named at birth.

Fatima uses her African name most of the time. She has not had it changed legally but had a community naming ceremony nearly twenty years ago. On the subject of her name she says:

> My name, I should say was imposed on me when I started working at the shule. After being there for like a half a year, they would change . . . you would get your name changed unless you just had a real objection to it. I had looked at different names at other times I had adopted names but I didn't really think, it never stuck until I had the naming ceremony in December of 1976. And I, listening to the name, it was about a month after I received the name that I really started to like it . . . It means respect and honor me. I mean the meaning was like, oh boy, you have alot to live up to here, you know. So it was, can you handle this mantle that's being bestowed upon you? I never thought of myself like that. So it was interesting to see what other people, you know, thought of you.

Nuessel (1992) writes:

> One traditional symbol of oppression is the imposition of a name on the person or group of people subjugated. The ability to name is a symbolic gesture that grants to the namer the power to tyrannize. Thus most

> liberation movements seek to wrest this important tool of domination from the despots who wield it. This, of course, was a reaction to the racist naming patterns of white slave owners who often chose names for their slaves that were intended to demean and ridicule them . . . As a reaction to centuries of racism, we see in the Black power movement of the 1960's a trend toward individual renaming in order to signify newfound freedom.

Barbara, the participant who prefers being called African, not Black, Afro-American or African-American, does not use an African name. When we discussed the issue of name changes she said:

> I am in favor of changing names legally to African names. I have an African name but I do not use it in public. But until I am ready to do it legally and forever . . . I don't feel comfortable with the dichotomy the way some people do. I am in favor of dismissing slave names and replacing them with names selected to describe character.

Considering the fact that she dresses in African attire 95% of the time and has made the decision to wear her hair in locks, as described in the previous section, I was somewhat surprised by, what I perceived to be, her ambivalence on the name change issue.

Ambivalence was an attitude that was not at all prevalent in the discussions I had with the participants on religion. Most of the participants had very definite feelings on the subject. In the next section, I will explore their thoughts on organized religion and spirituality.

African-American Self Concept Defined in Terms of Religion

The African-American church has traditionally been a source of strength and stability in the African-American community. DuBois (1903) wrote that "the Negro church of today is the social center of Negro life in the United States and the most characteristic expression of African character." One way or another, religion has been an important part of the lives of each of the participants. In some cases religion has motivated and continues to motivate the activism of the individuals involved in this study. In other cases, the perceived hypocrisy of the church has pushed participants away from organized religion and towards a more general spirituality.

Asante (1988) writes that the church has served both as dissuader and catalyst in our most necessary social and political struggles. This concept is supported throughout participant interviews. From my experience, many African-Americans outside of the nationalist community believe that somehow the tenets of African-American nationalism—namely the association with Africa, the belief in self-determination for African-American people regarding names, hairstyles, attire andspirituality— are anti-Christian. A recent personal experience will illustrate my point.

I was engaged in a conversation with an African-American woman in her early sixties and a self-proclaimed Christian. She is now working through a senior citizen association and has been placed as a clerical assistant at a African-American nationalist school. At this school, the adult men and women are referred to as 'Baba' and 'Mama', respectively plus their first names. What follows is her explanation of her train of thought. She is unhappy at the institution because she believes that the people here are not Christian and not to be Christian is wrong. She assumed that the school community was Muslim because people there refer to one another as Mama or Baba or Sister or Brother. She believes that "this whole Africa thing is just stupid." She also mentioned believing most of the things that Malcolm X said but that she could not fully respect him because his religion was wrong. In fact, Mama and Baba are Kiswahili words for mother and father respectively. The children spend up to eleven hours per day at the school. An effort is made for them to feel that the school staff is family and the should be treated as such and respected as such. Even in the African-American Protestant churches in America, parishioners are referred to as sister and brother so-and-so.

The unity of the African-American community is truly in jeopardy when we lack respect for one another based on religious differences. The fear that some African-American Christians who are not a part of the nationalist community seem to have is that one cannot be a nationalist and a good Christian at the same time. The commonly held belief seems to be that African-American nationalists hate European Americans and doctrines of hate are not in keeping with the Christian faith. By the same token, in my experience many people in the African-American nationalist community have an automatic bias against proclaimed Christians, believing that they are passive and lack commitment to radical change for African-Americans.

What follows is a discussion of the different roles religion has played in the lives of selected African-American activists.

Most participants fell in to the middle ground territory in terms of religion. There were no self-proclaimed atheists in the group nor were there any interviews that reflected extreme religious fervor. One participant stood out from the rest in that the focus of his activism is the African-American church. He discussed in great detail the potential that he believes exists within this institution for the capacity to change the lives of the African-American masses. John comments:

> I'd like to be one of the people out there getting ministers to stop and take a look and say wait a minute, look at your congregation. I mean, who are you servicing there. Do you really have those people in there who are out there making a difference . . . and I think for the most part, I think that the people who are making things happen, both positively and negatively, in the neighborhoods are doing it through the churches.

When Gertrude talked about the role of the church in her upbringing, she speaks of a "very democratic upbringing." Her mother belonged to the African Methodist Episcopal (AME) church. Gertrude says of this church:

> My mother was Methodist, she was AME. I studied the Negro history and when I found out there had been a revolt, that the African Methodist Episcopal had actually revolted from the church because they had not been allowed to worship, you know, with the whites in the congregation, but had been isolated in some rafter of the church and you know treated like they didn't belong . . . I was very happy to have, you know to identify with a religion that had that kind of tradition.

Gertrude's mother allowed her to visit various churches to decide where she felt most comfortable. Her mother did not go to church frequently. Gertrude explains:

> I was made to understand that church going was not necessarily an indication of one's spirituality and I did hear conversation in the adult community about the hypocrites who go to church all the time but don't do any of the things they claim to believe.

Gertrude raises the very important issue of religion versus spirituality. Denise also talks in terms of being spiritual.

> But from a personal standpoint, my knowledge of my relationship with the Father is very important. And I think more so now than anything else, I realize that I am more spiritual. I'm a spiritual being making my journey. And I find that it makes day to day living easier for me because I know that certain situations, I can transform because I take them to my Father. And I'm learning daily to take them to Him and leave them there.

Kwame acknowledges the presence of religion in his upbringing, but expresses the doubts he has in the church. He talks about how the enjoyment of going to church was almost entirely based on its social aspects:

> I used to go to Sunday School regularly, all the things you do as part of the activity of church, But I never really got into it, so when I got the first opportunity I moved away from the church. I still believe in the Creator, although I have difficulty understanding how the kinds of things that go on in this society . . . but I do believe that someone, more powerful than us, created what we have here.

Fatima talks about leaving the organized church based on the hypocrisy she observed and Hasani concurs. When asked about the role of religion in his upbringing he states:

> I came out of the Baptist church, spent some time in the Methodist church and a little bit of time in the Roman Catholic church. But, I think the major part, it at least began to speak to me more and more. But I left the church because of the hypocrisy. Just so much, you know, in all areas. And I just did not want to be a part of that. I do think the values are important and I try to instill them in our children. But we pull our values from our culture and so forth.

Fatima states that even when she was participating in organized religion, it had very little impact on her life:

> Well there was a Presbyterian church. That was the nearest church so we went there. And finally, I guess when I was about ten, they opened up a Baptist church near us so I started going there. My father wasn't real religious. My mother was, I mean I shouldn't say that. My mother didn't go to church that often but she wanted us to go to Sunday school and church. And I was a Sunday school secretary and in the choir. So we, you know, we participated . . . Just the hypocrisy of the church, you know, I saw as a young teenager turned me off.

Fatima said that she wouldn't even have mentioned the church had I not asked her about it. However, later in her interview when she talked about future goals, she mentioned spiritual goals.

> I'm probably going to move to a structured community, like the Yoruba community. That seems to kind of touch me more than anything right now. So, I'm going to start doing some study and talking to people who are in the community.

Karimah also speaks to the role of religion in her life. She states:

> I don't believe in organized religion. I believe that there is a God and God is the Creator and the Creation is the Bible as far as I'm concerned. But I don't disrespect any religion. I've studied them all. I've been to churches, synagogues, ashrans. I've been to all of them and they all have validity for those people who believe. But for me beliefs are best shown through your actions.

As is demonstrated by the words of the participants, the church most certainly played a role in the lives of most, whether for the positive or negative. Most acknowledge a level of spirituality in their lives and at the same time reject organized religion.

I would hesitate to say, in the cases of the participants in this study, that their concepts of themselves as African-Americans came largely from the church. The major factor in forming a positive African-American self concept seems to have come from the family. In the next section, I will discuss the participants thoughts regarding their families as they relate to the formation of their concepts of themselves.

African-American Self Concept Defined in Terms of Family

In this section, I will follow the suggestion of Foster (1983), as Littlejohn-Blake and Darling (1993) did. Foster writes:

> The traditional method of studying families has often focused on the pathological rather that on the strong family. However, accentuating positive aspects could prove to be more important in a long term basis than simply solving problems and weathering crises. Understanding the strengths of families has great potential for helping to solve many of the problems that families incur.

Family values are an important determinant of an individuals life chances. But, contrary to belief of many, the nuclear family is not the only kind of family that can effectively transmit strong family values. This is demonstrated again and again in my discussions with the participants.

Argyle (1968) writes about three major influences on the development of self concept. The first is communication directly from other people about the self. The second is the comparison of self with others in the immediate environment. The third influence is the role assigned to the self by one's community. Wyne (1974) suggests that the home and family life play a major role as the source of each of Argyle's bases for establishing a self image.

> In the home, the individual frequently receives direct communication from other family members about his self. Further, he consistently uses these family members as yardsticks to measure his development of self, and finally, the position of the home, both geographically and socially, in the community determines in part the role assigned to the self by the family members. In fact, the black lower-class home has been described as the "crucible of identity (Rainwater, 1966), suggesting perhaps that the individual's identity is, figuratively speaking, tested out or molded within the environs of the home. (Wyne, 1974)

A strong family support system was a recurrent theme in participant interviews in terms of to what they attributed their current places in life. Families were described in a variety of ways and in only 4 out of 11 cases was the nuclear family, consisting at minimum of a mother, father and child, among the descriptions. The focus was placed not on the makeup of the family, but on the level of support and love given by that family.

This is a crucial point because it speaks to the issue of the life chances of so many African-American children who do not live as part of a nuclear family. Some would like to attribute the problems being faced by and caused by these children to the absence of a father in their lives or more specifically, in their homes. I would support the idea that **one** of the best possible scenarios may be a loving, caring mother and a loving, caring father raising a child or children together in the same home. However, as the participants have proven by being living examples, the nuclear family may be one positive situation but not the only effective one.

> I was a dad's girl. I loved my dad. In fact, just thinking about him and talking about the fact that I was born, I haven't really thought about him in a little while. He's been dead now about 13 years. And I loved him so much for so long. And I hurt so much because he left us when I was 10 years old. And it just changed my life around because my dad worked, he worked for a railroad. Although we lived in Ida B. Wells projects I had a mom and a dad and my dad had a job. And on the other

> hand I had my grandma and my grandad. So I just had, I had everything. And I didn't know at the time that I had everything.

Even though Denise was devastated by her father's leaving the family, she survived emotionally because of the strength of the family that remained. Her father had such a powerful impact on her life. She did not dwell on what she may have missed by not having her father around. In fact she credits him with being her motivation to achieve:

> . . . but he made me want to be more, be more than people expect. Because you know, I didn't know on growing up Dia that being African-American, because we were colored in those days, you really didn't expect anything. Whatever you did was okay.

Denise married and divorced early and put off her education because of this. But, due to a supportive family structure, she returned to school and earned Bachelors and Masters degrees in English and Urban Studies respectively. Based on the experiences of this study's participants, a strong family support system can make a positive difference. Motivation from family does not necessarily come from parents or older role models. Malome and Karimah both verbalized the influence their children had upon them. Karimah says of her daughter: "so she became the center of my being and my reason for being and my reason for working and all of that. And so she still, still is."

Malome speaks in equally passionate terms with regard to his daughter and how her birth changed his life.

> I guess I've got to talk about what it means to be a parent and what role that has played in my eagerness and commitment to education. **As I said, when my daughter was born it was like a rebirth for me. I really stopped being the old person that I was and became a new person when she was born . . . she was a driving force.** I remember doing things like spending my last dime to get formula or whatever it was that she needed. And I remember feeling I would never have done that before (laughter), for anybody other than me !

To conclude, I will assert that the largest component in the development of a positive African-American self concept for the participants in this study was the influence of the family. Argyle (1968) would probably not be surprised, as he believed that communication from others and comparison of self with others in the immediate environment are two of the major factors that affect an individual's concept of him or her self.

The influence of the family was not only in terms of the positive. In two cases, with Hasani and Denise, a parent played an important positive role early in each of their lives, but left under negative circumstances. In Hasani's case, his mother introduced him to African-American literature in his early teens, but died a drug abuser. In Denise's case, her father was always the rock in her life but after divorcing her mother, did not maintain contact with his children. During their interviews, each of them expressed, on a very subtle level, succeeding despite the loss of a parent under negative circumstances. In fact, each attributed some of their motivation to succeed to these negative life situations.

Four of the participants, Karimah, Malome, Denise and Gertrude, attributed much of their motivation to do well in life and to persevere beyond adverse conditions to the births of their children.

Three of the participants, Hakim, Fatima, and Oba, specifically cited the families by whom they were raised as supportive and deserving of credit for their respective stations in life.

So, the influence of the family came in a variety of forms. Some of the motivating circumstances were negative, some were positive and from the parents and some participants were motivated by their offspring. In some cases, the positive influence of the family came in the form in which is traditionally expected, i.e. the loving parents. In other cases, the influence came later through the participants roles as loving parents. In whatever form it came for these participants, it was powerful and memorable enough for them to discuss it with me, in many cases, 20 or more years after the fact.

In the next section, I will discuss the role that the formal schooling experiences played in the lives of these participants with regard to their self concept.

African-American Self Concept as Defined through Formal Schooling Experiences

In this section, I will discuss how some of the formal schooling experiences have affected the African-American self concept of the participants. Malome states:

> The first day I was in the third grade in the white school, the first comment that the white teacher made to me was 'shutup, I don't know what you people used to do at Dunbar, but we don't do that here'. You see, we were scattered across town and whereas we had been in a class where it was all African-American children, we suddenly found ourselves in a situation where we were in a class of 25 or 30 students and there were only like three or four of us. We were a distinct minority. Everything was geared to the white students. In our third grade song book there were two songs that whenever we had music we had brought our book to sing. One song that was in the book was 'Old Black Joe' and the other was 'Jenny Cracked Corn'. Jenny Cracked Corn had a picture of an enslaved African woman picking cotton or something to go along with the song and had this picture of an old bald headed man with white hair, a conventional uncle Ben looking type person to go along with the Old Black Joe song. Can you imagine not knowing any better and sitting in the class and the teacher pulling out the book and saying 'turn to page 74 and let's sing Old Black Joe? And there we are in the class and we're embarrassed and not knowing what to do. And that hurt !!

What we see here is how an individual's sense of self can be negatively affected by a curriculum that devalues his culture. Pinar (1993) talks about curriculum as being one highly significant form of representation and arguments over curriculum are also arguments over who we are as Americans, including how we wish to represent ourselves to our children; what we want them to think we are and who they might become.

Kwame also had experiences in elementary school that could have been very detrimental to self concept. He admits to having been a behavioral problem. However, on occasion, even when the discussion was engaging enough to invoke his participation, he didn't always receive a positive reaction:

> I remember when I was in the 5th grade my math teacher, when talking about parallel lines, she said railroad tracks meet down the road. And of course they don't meet down the road, they appear to meet. I blurted out, "that's a lie, railroad tracks never meet." I got suspended for that and that was the first time I got suspended and my mother had to come up to school. So I had a number of experiences like that.

The formal schooling experiences of the participants had an affect on their development as African-Americans. Malome was in a newly desegregated school system. Kwame's teacher, may not have been prepared or inclined to deal with the energy of an African-American boy. Their experiences were somewhat different than those participants who were formally educated in a segregated system. Generally the experiences of the latter were more positive in terms of helping to develop a positive African-American self concept. John attended an historically African-American college. Of this experience he says:

> So I went to——and I played one year of football and I played four years of baseball. And———,—that was a very nurturing experience because the teachers there were interested in the students. They knew you by name. They kept close tabs and they communicated well with your parents when they came down to visit. So that's what I needed at the time because I was a young man. I was never in trouble, but I was a young man then who didn't realize at that time that I, I didn't even know what leadership was. I never thought about it.

Hakim also attended an historically African-American college. He speaks specifically about the effect of that experience on his self concept:

> So when I went off to college I went to —— in ——, ——. It was a real tremendous opportunity being in a Black environment. I chose to go to —— and became immersed in Black culture. So I worked with Black students from across the country. I had a very good undergrad experience, totally immersed in Blackness. I was involved with alot of

> activities on campus. So I grew and developed in terms of my consciousness and capabilities and feelings of self worth.

Growth is an important concept in this research. Each of the participants has expressed the concept in his or her own way. Some call it growth, some, development. I will refer to it as transformation. In the next section I will discuss the participants transformations to intellectual-activism and how that transformation was influenced by their experiences as described previous chapters.

The Transformation to a Positive African-American Self Concept

Introduction

As many human beings have, each of the participants has experienced a struggle to attain significance and meaning in their lives each in his or her own way. A positive African-American self concept and a feeling of significance in one's life are each a part of what enables each of the participants to work successfully in and for the African-American community. The previous sections have detailed the ways in which participants define themselves in terms of nationalism and Afrocentricity, religion and family. The following section will be a discussion of some specific turning points that have led the participants to live their lives as they are today. I will use the participants own words to demonstrate how particular events in their lives led them to define themselves as African-Americans and the goals that they have set to guide their lives.

The idea of knowing oneself and the importance one's Blackness plays in that self knowledge is supported by Na'im Akbar (1982). He writes that to know oneself in relation to one's Blackness is to have a true education as opposed to a miseducation. Among African-Americans, a positive self concept is often dependent upon acceptance of some very basic physical facts such as skin color and hair texture. Not surprisingly, this rang especially true with the female participants in this study. This was expected due to the stringent beauty standards that are applied to women in the United States.

Participant Turning Points

Turning points are important because they facilitate major change. They represent an individual coming to the realization that in life there is choice. They really boil down to the power of having options. Options exist in every situation. One option may not be much better than the next, but there are choices to be made never-the-less. There is something very liberating about knowing that there is always another way.

Turning points can be positive or negative. I will focus on the positive ones for the purpose of this study.

Although turning points often involve other people, they are fundamentally very personal. The feeling that you've moved to another level is what essentially defines a turning point. During each of the interviews I conducted, there was always a mention of one or more turning points, or an event or series of events in one's life that guides one toward a different course in life, to another level. A turning point is a transformation of sorts. Transformations can have physical manifestations, but all take place in the mind.

Karimah's comments are supported by Wyne's (1974) defense of the need to study the African-American self specifically; "the fact that the self image of black Americans is fundamentally related to a color caste system justifies exclusive treatment of the topic."

The idea of a positive African-American self concept is important to this study in terms of how that self concept is developed. The various components that contribute to the development process such as family, spirituality, role models and formal educational experiences will be highlighted in the following sections.

It is important for me to know how each of the participants came to value his or her Blackness and place it as the cornerstone for self definition. The placement of Blackness as the center of oneself is the common tie that binds this group of participants. If the purpose of this study is to be achieved, my analysis must reveal such common ties in order to develop a foundation for the creation on a new generation of African-Americans that work, in whatever way they feel is best, for the liberation and progress of African-American people.

In this section I will discuss the idea of a African-American self concept as defined by Wyne (1974), the difference between how the participants perceive themselves as compared to how they are seen by others and finally, how self concept among the majority population differs fundamentally from self concept among African-Americans.

How an individual defines him or her self is important in this study. Participants were chosen based on how they are seen within the African-American community. However, how one is seen can differ greatly from how one sees oneself.

> The primary concern self measurement should not be with what the "real self" is but rather with how the individual perceives himself, since reality is not necessarily a determinant of an individual's self concept. (Wyne, 1974, pg. 11)

Wyne's point surfaced on many occasions throughout my interviews with participants. All of the participants involved in the study are perceived by others as African-American nationalists. As the data will show, most of the participants prefer not to align themselves that closely with the African-American nationalist community, for reasons which will be discussed in more detail in a later section. With or without the label of African-American nationalist, each of the participants wanted and found meaning and significance in their lives through their work in the African-American community. Part of wanting to work to make a difference in the African-American community comes from having a positive African-American self concept. At the same time, making a positive difference in the community contributes to the positive African-American self concept of the worker.

In the next section, I will discuss the struggle for significance as defined by Brennecke and Amick (1975) and the kind of significance the participants in this study have achieved and for which they continue to struggle.

In this section, I will discuss the process of Afrocentric transformations. developing a positive concept of selfhood and the "struggle for significance," as outlined by Brennecke and Amick (1975), that is often a part of that process. I will go further to discuss the process of developing a self concept as it relates specifically to the African-American community.

Asante (1988) discusses transformation specific to African-American people. The process he describes consists of five stages skin recognition, environmental recognition, personality awareness, interest-concern and culminates in Afrocentric awareness. He defines Afrocentric awareness as the point at which a person becomes totally changed to a conscious level in the involvement of the struggle for his or her own mind liberation and that only when this happens can we say that a person is aware of the collective conscious will. What Asante says next speaks to my idea of turning points being a realization of power. He states "an imperative of will, powerful, incessant, alive and vital moves to eradicate every trace of powerlessness . . . Afrocentricity is like rhythms; it dictates the beat of your life !"

Fanon (1963) writes about three phases involved in the evolution to national consciousness for what he terms the native intellectual. In the first phase, the native intellectual demonstrates that he has assimilated the culture of the occupying power. Fanon has labeled this first phase unqualified assimilation. He describes the second phase as one in which the native intellectual is disturbed and decides to remember who he is. In the third and final phase, which Fanon labels the fighting phase, the native intellectual becomes an awakener of the people and the "mouthpiece of a new reality in action."

Although participants may not label themselves Afrocentric, by Asante's definition and my analysis, each is experiencing a process of personal transformation in the direction of Afrocentricity. What follows is a discussion of participants' experiences, many of which reflect the various levels of Afrocentric transformation as described by Asante. In the following accounts by participants, each of the turning points involved others but were very personal experiences.

"As human beings unfold like flowers blossoming from nub to bud into full blown flowerhood, they become conscious of who and what they are." (Brennecke, 1975, pg. 9) What follows is a description of the transformations and turning points of the participants. After these transformations and turning points, some of them arrived at African-American nationalism, some at pan-Africanism, some at an unlabeled state, all at a positive African-American self concept. I have discussed the roles of religion, family upbringing and environment in the lives of each of the participants. I have also discussed their feelings about African-American nationalism. However each of the participants have come to define themselves, they are all actively taking part in affecting the African-American community for the better. Their turning points represent the changes and growth within their lives that have contributed to their dedication to the survival and uplift of the African-American community. Hasani mentioned two very specific turning points in his life and what follows is a very passionate description.

> My mother, when I was around 13, had asked me to go to the library and get a book by Richard Wright. And reading Richard Wright was like lamps on in my head because this was the first time I had heard anything or read anything positive about Black people. And of course there were negative qualities in the book too, but that we could write a book and publish it was new to me . . . **And so what at least began to put me on the road to a life that I'm in today was the discovery of Black literature and the power of ideas.**

This discussion struck me as very powerful because in a world of physical violence, here is a African-American teen-aged boy discovering the **power of ideas.** In the United States, power tends to be equated to financial assets; primarily money and property. Many African-American children have bought into that concept, like many others living in America. While substitute teaching in a second grade class room, I asked the children to draw a picture of what they wanted to be when they grew up. One picture gave me such an emotional reaction that I had to excuse myself for a brief moment. This 7 year old boy had drawn a detailed portrait of himself as a drug dealer, complete with drugs, weapons and no shortage of money (see appendix 1.1). When I got home that afternoon, I wept uncontrollably. A baby, a seven year old baby, dreamt and fantasized about a "profession" that is destroying the African-American community. A "profession" that makes me apprehensive in a neighborhood that only 10 years before I walked freely and without reservation. Everything in his little world said loudly and clearly that power is "who has the biggest gun" or "who sells the most drugs" or "who has the biggest, most extravagant car" or "who has the most money." How was I to convince *this* child that the real power was in ideas? This is a way in which this study can have practical applications. Certainly, every turning point for the interviewees may not be a turning point for every second grade boy, but for the sake of the survival of the African-American community, its surely worth a try.

Malome also experienced a turning point brought on by a particular event. In his case the event took place on a college campus:

> As soon as I saw a Black Student Union meeting, I went to that. And that meeting marked the point of my consistent involvement in the movement, the struggle. Because from that day forward, I was always involved.

This was a positive experience with Malome. At least one participant expressed a negative experience that she was able to turn into a positive turning point. Fatima experienced some very serious emotional turmoil in her teen years involving her family. She states that "I knew I wouldn't advance as a person until I left the city." Her move was the beginning of a transformation for her. Below she speaks of her evolution:

> Coming to ——, because when I came to —— I decided I was going to become involved in the nationalist organization. Before that I had been involved with Black community organizations . . . It was the reading I was doing, the political reading. It was all this internal stuff. It wasn't that I was you know, felt this anger at white folks or anything. Just in reading and analyzing things. I was reading, you know, Eldridge Cleaver. I was reading some of the things the Panther Party put out and I was reading for like poetry. I was attending cultural events and just, it was like an evolution I guess.

The "American Dream" of not only financial stability but luxury and excess is promoted as ideal for all American children via television and other forms of media. For some children, this dream seems very reasonable. As they grow older, these same children probably begin to feel that it's only a matter of time before they take their places as keepers of this dream. For many children, however, in more impoverished communities they have experienced only three types of people; people who do not work and have no money; people who work and live from paycheck to paycheck, hand to mouth; and those who engage in illegal activities and have lots of money. One of the reasons that I believe that many of these children do not see the full spectrum of people, including people who have worked hard and are living comfortably, is because these people usually move out of the neighborhood and therefore out of the view of the children who most need to see them on a daily basis. One of the reasons for my choice of participants was the factor of community visibility. I realized through my discussions with participants that **visibility** was one of the things I looked for consistently but subconsciously. This is not to say that in order to be effective, an activist must be physically visible because, of course, people donate money all the time. This money serves a purpose and is an "old stand by" in terms of an effective, efficient way to contribute to a cause. However, money cannot be a role model, a caring voice or a sympathetic ear. Money cannot be the encouraging chat or a thought provoking commentary that motivates so many African-Americans to make positive steps in their lives.

The other turning point mentioned by Hasani occurred during his time in the military service. At this point in his life,he had begun to do a great deal of reading. He was already leaning toward the path of activism and the following occurrence confirmed his choice to work for the uplift of African-Americans:

> On the way to basic training I was reading a book by Paul Robeson, Here I Stand, and when we got to basic training and I had the book when I got off the bus. The drill sergeant saw Paul Robeson's face on the book and snatched the book from my hand and said 'what's yo' Negro ming doing reading this Black communist'. So he told all the recruits to line up against the bus. And he took the book and held it with

> his hand and tore the pages out and gave the pages to each recruit and told them to use it for toilet paper.

Each of these turning points had an effect on the way the individual feels about himself as an African-American. Either positively or negatively, the turning points described affect the African-American self concept.

Turning points can be initiated by the individual, or inadvertently by others (as with Hasani, who was inspired by African-American literature). Either way, they are powerful circumstances that have long term effects. They are liberating because in many ways they say to the individual, you have options. The power of choice is massive. There is probably nothing more depressing than being in a bad situation and feeling that there is no way out. This discovery of the power of choice was also discussed by Kwame:

> So I had no real thoughts of going to college at that time. I was just going to work on Wall Street. Then I realized that after two years on Wall Street, I had reached as high as I could reach without a degree. Aside from the Blacks on Wall Street who were officers in forms or the guys who buy stocks for people . . . brokers, I was about the highest ranking Black person there. What I didn't like about corporate America is that I didn't see any Black people doing anything of significance. **So in a sense, that was a starting point to my understanding of Black/white relations.** I hadn't decided to leave. I would have been at this place the following year if this situation hadn't developed with Oberlin College. But I was beginning to get frustrated and realize that I wasn't going anywhere !

Here again, the idea of a turning point relates to the realization of the power of choice; the idea that there's something more out there, something that takes one to another level. This turning point also addresses the African-American self concept of Kwame. He was bothered by the positions held by African-Americans and this affected the way he saw himself in terms of his own career as an African-American.

Turning points/transformations are a sign of growth. Talk show host Oprah Winfrey said in an interview that she has no regrets in her life, even of the most horrendous crimes against her, including her molestation and rape by family members. She explains that all of those events made her who she is today. She went on to say that she may not have been able to handle other difficult situations she faces had she not been forced to endure her past. Another participant concurs. Denise says:

> In the seventies I went through a divorce. And all these things, Dia, they change you. They work on you. You know, you hear only the strong survive. I thought my dad's leaving was hard. I thought being on Public Aid was hard. I thought not having what others had was hard, because now by the time my dad left , we were starting to buy cars and things like that. But nothing prepared me for going through this divorce. **I guess in my own way I was planning on doing something else. And I found out when I committed myself to find out, that the seventies brought alot of this on !**

What seems to separate these participants and others like them from those who do not fare well in life is that in times of adversity, they do not fall, they rise. If they do happen to fall temporarily, they take a lesson from the situation and make the most of it. This is a sign of having a positive self concept. The ability to move forward from a difficult situation is one manifestation of self confidence.

Over and over again, evidence of the stages described by Asante (1988) surfaced in participant interviews. Every participant does not necessarily experience each stage of any of the three transformation models (Asante, 1988, Freire, 1970 and Fanon, 1963). The stages experienced by each participant were heavily dependent upon several factors, particularly the kind of environment in which they were raised. Hasani says:

> . . . Both my parents were very strong in their racial beliefs. So I was always inspired to stand up for what I believed in and not feel inferior regardless of the fact that there were few Blacks in public school and almost no Black teachers and things like that. But my church upbringing and close family ties gave me the encouragement to pretty much do the best you can to try and stand up for your beliefs.

Hasani was raised to feel good about his Blackness. Much of the heartache felt by many African-Americans, due to a negative African-American self concept, was avoided in Hasani's case and in the case of Oba.

Oba also talks about the activism in his family that helped to shaped his attitudes about African-American people and himself as an African-American man.

> My father sort of set the atmosphere in the home. Very serious, hard working and very committed to helping people. So those qualities he possessed I had observed very young. My father was also a self taught artist, and a sculptor of note and he was highly respected in the art community. And when you grow up in that kind of environment, it rubs off.

Conclusion

In analyzing this research, the idea of a positive African-American self concept was key for two general and interrelated reasons: 1) it was an underlying theme in all participant interviews and therefore 2) it may very well be the key to cultivating a new generation of activists.

I open this chapter by using the theory of symbolic interactionism to demonstrate the existence, importance and uniqueness of symbols used in the African-American community as exemplified by the participants in this study and how these symbols contribute to the African-American self concept. The concept of the Black self as developed by Wyne (1974) was used to describe what it means to have a positive African-American self concept. Wyne's concept was used a the basis for the discussion on factors that contribute to the African-American self concept.

Throughout the chapter, discussion by the participants is used to support the assertions; 1) that each of the participants possess a positive African-American self concept, 2) that they used symbols of their Blackness to communicate their positive African-American self concepts to themselves and to others and that 3) the fact that each of the participants has a positive African-American self concept has given each the desire to work for the liberation an uplift of African-American people. In their introduction to *Significance: the struggle we share*, Brennecke and Amick write:

> To feel significant is not necessarily to become important or famous; far from it. Most people to whom this book is addressed will never become famous or wealthy or powerful. But they can attain a feeling of significant selfhood. They can live their lives in such a full and rewarding way that they will come to know that their being here has mattered, that they have made a ripple on the pond. (pg. ix)

The pond for the participants in this study is the African-American community. In the next chapter on goals of activism and progress toward those goals, I will discuss the ways in which this group has madeits ripple in the form of the liberation and uplift of African-American people.

VI
Progress Towards Goals of Activism

Introduction

In chapter four, I described the background of each of the participants in this study. Each of the background descriptions of the participants explains how they fit the criteria of African-American intellectual-activist and how I came to choose each of them for this research. In chapter five, I discussed the major tie that binds each of the participants; the possession of a positive African-American self concept. This discussion included the definition of a positive African-American self concept and was framed within the context of two theories; Wyne's (1974) work on the Black self and Brennecke's and Amick's (1975) work on selfhood and significance.

In this chapter, I will discuss how the combination of a positive Black self concept and the struggle for significance has shaped the lives of the participants in this study in three major ways; 1) by placing them in a frame of mind that highlights their Blackness as the driving force in their lives, 2) by moving them to work for the uplift of African-American people and 3) by leading them to establish purposes for their lives that are inextricably linked to the progress of African-American people.

I will present the life purposes of the participants as they were described to me. Further, I will document what they see as progress for the African-American community and how they see their activism as contributing to this progress.

Statement of Life Purposes and Goals of Activism

Introduction

"There can be no progress without struggle"

Frederick Douglas

What is considered progress? Is it when we, as African-Americans have our own schools, hospitals, neighborhoods and businesses to support all our needs and desires. Or is it when we not only have access to but respect within European-American schools, hospitals, neighborhoods and businesses. Integration versus segregation, integration versus separation, integration versus independence. What are the goals of our activism?

One of the main goals expressed by the participants in this study was choice. The idea that if we want to build our own schools, we should be free to do so, but if we choose to move into a neighborhood that is primarily European, we should be able to do that freely as well. These are the choices Europeans have always been able to make.

Cornel West (1993) describes two camps when discussing the plight of African-Americans. He labels one camp liberal structuralists. He says that those in this camp highlight structural constraints on the life chances of Black people. They call for full employment, health, education and child care programs and broad affirmative action practices. He labels those in the other camp conservative behaviorists. They support self-help programs, Black business expansion and non-preferential job practices. They are all very much in favor of doing for self. Self includes the literal self, family and the larger African-American community. Certainly they are not against government programming but all believe in the Seven Principles of Blackness or the Nguzo Saba developed by Dr. Maulana Karenga (1988). The principles, along with their English translations are as follows: **Umoja** - Unity: To strive for and maintain unity in the family, community, nation and race. **Kujichagulia** — Self Determination: To define ourselves, create for ourselves and speak for ourselves. **Ujima**—Collective Work and Responsibility: To build and maintain our community together and to make our brothers' and sisters' problems our problems and solve them together. **Ujamaa** —Cooperative Economics: To build and maintain our own stores, shops and others businesses and to profit from them together. **Nia**— Purpose: To make as our collective vocation the building and developing of our community in order to restore our people to their traditional greatness. **Kuumba** — Creativity: To do always as much as we can in the way that we can in order to leave our community more beautiful and beneficial than when we inherited it. **Imani** — Faith: To believe with all our hearts in our parents, our teachers, our leaders, our people and the righteousness and victory of our struggle.

West (1993) goes on to discuss the limitations of each of the camps. He writes that the liberal structuralists ignore the structure of culture and concentrate solely on the economic and political structures as they relate to the African-American community. He criticizes the conservative behaviorist for ignoring the role of politics and the economy in the current state of African-American affairs.

The participants generally reflect, but are not limited to, the tenets of both camps. This is evident in the structure of their own lives. Although among them there is a concentration on changing the African-American community from within, they certainly realize that the structure of societal institutions are problematic, where African-Americans are concerned, and need to be addressed.

They have, however, gone beyond the ideals of the conservative behaviorists in that they fully acknowledge the victimization of people of African descent *and* act as agents for change within the community. This agency is a defining component in their activism and is related to the goals therein.

The goals of the participants fell into three major categories; children, raising consciousness and economic and cultural development and independence. The remainder of the chapter will follow these categories. Although I have arranged the chapter in this way, it should be understood that the categories are not mutually exclusive. For the most part, the collective opinion of the participants is that we should raise consciousness through the children for the purpose of economic and cultural development and independence.

Children

"Children are the reward of life"— African Proverb

It is apparent that each of the participants has a high level of commitment to the children of the African-American community as each of them had or has a career working directly with children. Gertrude says:

> . . . So I get up everyday knowing that somehow I got to align myself with like minded people and get them to become involved with the children, whether they want to become formally involved and actually go get into a program or what have you, but I just don't want to ever allow anybody to forget that it is the children for whom we are responsible and we have no other work that is more important than the children. The interesting thing about it is that we don't have a choice because if we don't become involved with the children and bond with the children and prevent so many of our children from becoming alienated from us, we won't be able to live in a community with our own children. So I get up everyday knowing that I have to continue to do this.

Kwame expressed feeling an emotional high when working with children. He talks about the lack of commitment we as African-American people have to the education of our children.

> I feel that people view education as schooling and have expectations that can't be met. I strongly advocate making the distinction between education and schooling and I feel that as a people, we don't do that. We put too much faith in schooling that we don't control to make a difference in our children's lives.

In keeping with the pattern of each of the participants, he took action on his beliefs; he started an African-centered school in the middle of his junior year in college.

Karima, when asked about the goals of her activism responded:

> I've seen bits and pieces of it everywhere and that gives me hope. And when I see that we're still having children, that gives me hope. It also gives me a responsibility because the idea is to be and know who you are and to act out of that. That's the ideal. I am now going into elderhood and so that I become a role model or a teacher who could provide guidance to others who are coming along the way so that they may not make some of the same errors or they may get some information earlier because they can handle it earlier than when I got it.

Below, Hakim speaks of his feelings after having heard Dr. King speak a rally. He says:

> So I returned to ——, like others to their respective home towns and made a decision that probably one of the things that I could do to help my people was to get involved with teaching. And I observed the inequity of the Black students' achievement and had done practice teaching for a year, one day a week for a year to kind of get a feel for what was going on in the public schools. So when I saw just how bad it was, and feeling that I had something to contribute, I decided to go into teaching so I could be of greater aid to my community.

That rally took place in 1966. Hakim would remain a dedicated teacher for nearly 30 years. Fatima is also a committed educator of young children. She has been teaching at a particular African-centered elementary school for the past 8 years. She has been involved with African-centered education for over twenty years. She continuously spoke of her commitment to African children throughout her interview.

> Well, I don't see myself in the classroom forever. I see myself probably working as an educator forever. It might take a different form. It just might not be the classroom. You might see a body of work that I've done in terms of curriculum for ______, or curriculum, some text books or story books, those kinds of things. I'll probably be active all my life on some level.

Barbara talks about her activism in terms of young people as well.

> Just day by day trying to make sure that the people that I come in contact with, especially the young people, know that there is an opportunity for them to learn what they need to learn. And I think that's—my activism comes in that form.

A final quote from Gloria is a good summary of the collective feelings of the participants:

> But I just don't want to ever allow anybody to forget that it is the children for whom we are responsible and we have no other work that is more important than the children. The interesting thing about it is that we don't have a choice, because if we don't become involved with the children and bond with the children and prevent so many more of our children from becoming alienated from us, we won't be able to live in a community with our own children.

Raising Consciousness

Before anything can be accomplished with any group of people, those people need to be aware of what is happening. In order for African-Americans to make progress, they need know where from they want to progress and to where they want to progress. Denise focusses the goals of her activism on raising consciousness. She says:

> So I was not a private or a lieutenant then. But I'm a captain now because if I can save one Black, one African-American, put them on the right track so that even though they slip and fall, they don't linger there. Because it doesn't matter how often you fall. It's how fast it takes you to recover. As long as you can recover, you're still in the ballpark. **But we have to be made aware that the struggle is our responsibility and it doesn't matter where we go in the corporate ladder, how far up the corporate ladder, we're always going to be who we are.** The thing that I want though is to make certain that we bring one along. You know, if I do this then pass it on to someone else.

Of his goals for African-Americans, Kwame says:

> I think that the issue is the development of knowledge, understanding and respect for African-Americans and African-American culture. I think that we can demand nothing less than that. Also, I think that full and complete status in this society, that is, the elimination of our present 2nd class status in terms of employment, education, housing, the prison population . . . this has to be eliminated.

Kwame is confident that he is assisting African-Americans in reaching these goals through his work.

> Hence, virtually all of my research is practical in terms of trying to make improvements in the African-American community . . . So I see the practical utilization of my work and the actual research as being intricately tied together and its that connection that makes me enjoy what I'm doing.

Kwame believes that he and other African-Americans have certain responsibilities to do all that can be done in terms of learning about African-American people and African people in general. He feels that "we have a responsibility to agitate the system wherever we are." He does this in his capacity as a university professor in terms of helping to recruit more faculty of color. A theme that ran throughout Kwame's interview was the importance of practical application. He goes on to say:

> I don't think it's unreasonable to assume that an African-American scholar, or any scholar for that matter, can effectively meet the demands of the university and also meet the demands of their own community. I don;t think that those are necessarily incompatible tasks. I think that we are often led to believe that they are incompatible tasks by the university and perhaps by the society that those are incompatible tasks. But I don't see my usefulness as a faculty member as being of very much relevance if I could not combine that with a practical involvement in the community.

So, one theme of activism that clearly emerged from the participant interviews was the idea of placing children as the focus. Raising consciousness was also critical according to the participants. Another theme that was prominent and will be discussed in the next section was that of economic and cultural development. It was difficult to separate out these two areas of development because the participants saw them as very closely connected. Part of cultural development is working toward economic independence. In the next section, the participants speak to these issues.

Economic and Cultural Development and Independence

> "If it isn't about nationbuilding, it isn't about anything."—John Henrik Clarke (1992).

Nationbuilding is defined as "the conscious and focussed application of our people's collective resources, energies and knowledge to the task of liberating and developing the psychic and physical space that we identify as ours." (Akoto, 1992) Akoto goes on to describe issues involved in nationbuilding such as the development of behaviors, values, language, institutions and physical structures that elucidate our history and culture, concretize and protect the present and insure the future identity and independence of the nation. Economic and cultural development are crucial to nationbuilding.

Entrepreneurship has long been one of the main foci of Black nationalism. Sovereignty is the basis of Black nationalism. There are many levels of nationalism. Garveyites sought freedom from external control through a "back to Africa" movement. Many of today's African-American nationalists would simply like economic independence.

Hasani believes that part of his responsibility as an intellectual is to engage in liberating activities. He states:

> And these liberating activities can be something as small as recognizing your own faults and then trying to correct them. Or it can be something as large as trying to truly develop independent Black institutions in our community. So I'm saying that everybody can participate. You see liberation is how do you move form one level of oppression to how do you overcome that oppression. I'm saying that it is a liberating act to be

> able to go out in front of your own facility and just be able to say pick up the paper out from in front of the door, you see.

So Hasani talks about economic independence not only in practical terms, but in terms of the intangible mental and spiritual rewards of feeling ownership.

African-Americans make up a huge consumer group in this country. The goods consumed are usually not produced or even sold by African-Americans. This is something that many of the participants would like to change. Most of them are currently engaged in entrepreneurship. Several own and operate businesses as a sole means of financial support and all do **some** independent work such as educational consulting, seminar facilitation and teacher training. Although participation in entrepreneurship was not one of the conditions upon which I based my selection, most participants have this in common. John speaks of entrepreneurship on a more tangible level than Hasani did. John comments:

> . . . No longer can we tell youth to go to college, to get their education, graduate and look to work in some organization or in some institution and be successful. What I think we have to develop in young people now is they have to go to school and they have to develop themselves. But we need to look at young people who can create jobs . . . they must be able to create institutions and organizations that will help and assist themselves, our people and even others because we can't do it alone, but we must take care of ourselves first.
>
> We've got to ingrain in our kids to have, they must have an entrepreneur's spirit where they can create and where they can employ and assist their own people.

Latif and Latif (1994) would agree with John. They write that even though there are more educational and economic opportunities, our neighborhoods do not reflect African-American entrepreneurship. And that even though African-Americans have the potential for economic power, they feel powerless, amongst all the non-Black businesses in the community, to create jobs for other African-Americans.

John defines the goals of his activism as economic and cultural viability. He states:

> Whatever it is that it takes to make you economically viable so that you can live the kind of lifestyle that you have defined for yourself within reason is what I mean by economic viability.

He specifies, however, that economic viability is not sufficient in and of itself because there are particular ways in which people attain lifestyles that are illegal and/or immoral. He stresses that cultural viability should not suffer at the hands of economics. Of cultural viability he says:

> So by cultural viability I mean that a person, each person is aware of his or her own history; their music, their art, their poems, their culture. All of those things make up their culture.

He concludes by saying:

> So a person then should be economically and culturally viable and to me that should be the epitome of what life is all about.

In discussing the Nguzo Saba, Madhubuti (1973) writes "each principle is the protein that feeds the larger body. If you lose one element, the body weakens" (pg.81). Adherence to these Seven Principles of Blackness contributes to the economic and cultural viability discussed by John. Madhubuti implores us to "study and adjust to the Black Value System - it is a major step toward the unification and empowerment of Afrikan people (pg. 82)." He goes on to imply that Black nationalists must live the Nguzo Saba and that all Afrikan people will benefit from this move toward the development of a Black value system that cuts across known religious and political systems. The ideal for African-Americans in this scenario is the unification and empowerment of African people. Many of the participants have said this and in a variety of ways. For example, John's goal is the economic empowerment and independence of African-Americans. And interesting comment on Madhubuti's work is by Dr. Chancellor Williams. He commends the book for being "replete with innovative and thought provoking ideas which should lead us directly to the task before the Black race." He goes on to describe those two tasks as he sees them. The first is the task of achieving intellectual emancipation. The second, which jives with Woodson's (1933) thoughts regarding the need to translate leadership into service is " a movement away from the Black age of talking, to one of constructive action and planning." All of this is in keeping with Freire's (1970) concept of praxis; the combination of intellect or thought and action. This concept was an important part of what went in to my choice of participants.

Praxis, in essence, is what I've been referring to as activism throughout this analysis. There were several "thinkers" (people who philosophize and write about innovative concepts for facilitating change in neighborhoods, educational settings and other social institutions) available to be interviewed for this study. What impressed me most about those who were eventually chosen as participants is that they were all thinkers who are willing to act !

Progress Toward Life Purposes and Goals of Activism

Progress As Movement Toward the Ideal

In this section I will define progress and the variety of areas in which progress can be evaluated.

Over the years there has never really been total agreement on the definition of progress for African-American people. Have we made progress when we get to the point of be welcome in traditionally segregated settings such as schools, restaurants, country clubs and neighborhoods. Is progress having our own schools, restaurants, country clubs and neighborhoods. Or, is progress having the opportunity to choose?

For the purposes of the study, progress will be defined generally as movement toward the ideal. Ideal can be looked at and defined in a variety of different ways. Progress can be affected by forces both inside and out of the community working toward progress. I will discuss two major factors that can affect the progress of the African-American community: miseducation and the relationship between African-American intellectuals and the African-American masses.

We can determine how the participants define progress for African-Americans by studying what they see as the ideal condition for African-Americans and how they see their activism as contributing to the ideal. Ideal can be defined in terms of education, economics, spirituality, social status and many other areas too vast to list.

The ideal for the education of school-aged children might mean an African-centered, independent institution for one group of people or admission to the most prestigious European-American institution for another group. It might also mean improving public schools to a level at which all children have access to a superior quality education.

The ideal in terms of spirituality might be seen as becoming a born-again Christian to some African-Americans and accepting Islam to others.

The economic ideal could range from the independence that comes with entrepreneurship to the ability to purchase anything one chooses because of the security and salary of a job at an established European-American company.

The point is simply this; ideal can be defined in many different ways and on many different levels. How one defines ideal will determine how one defines progress. The participants in this study represented a variety of opinions on the definition of ideal and progress. This group included Christians, pan-Africanists, nationalists, entrepreneurs, multiculturalists, teachers, professors, administrators, mothers, fathers, husbands and wives. Each of these categories contributes to the way ideal and progress are seen.

An important distinction when analyzing the progress of the African-American community is how one defines oneself. For example, if one describes oneself as a Black nationalist, ones standards for progress are different than someone who, for example is an assimilationist. Therefore, the evaluation of what is successful may differ. For example: if an African-American high school senior is accepted at and chooses to attend a university such as Harvard, the assimilationist may see this as great progress where the Black nationalist might ask why not Howard or Tuskeegee or some other historically Black college or university. This example is in no way meant to imply that an assimilationist is the opposite of a Black nationalist. This example simply illustrates that the progress of African-Americans may be judged differently based on the self definition of the judge. This certainly rang true in the participant interviews. The ideals of those who defined themselves as Black nationalists were somewhat different from those who defined themselves otherwise.

Blackness as a Driving Force in the Definition of Ideal.

As was discussed in chapter on Black self concept, each of the participants has a positive one. Not only does each of them feel good about being Black, but their Blackness is the driving force in their lives; everything centers around the fact of their Blackness. It is important to note that this centeredness is a positive one. Hasani, when discussing his motivation to work for the African-American community states:

> But I think that the bottom line of all this is why I do this and why I continue to function and work in this area is quite simple : . . I love Black people ! And I don't see anything more important than the survival and development of our people. I don't see anything more important than that. Not my own personal wealth or safety or anything. I think that that means very little if we don't survive and develop as a people.

Hasani is one of the founders of one of themore established independent African-centered schools in this country. There are over forty schools registered with the Council of Independent Black Institutions (CIBI), a national governing body of independent Black schools. And certainly there are other schools of this nature that are unaffiliated with CIBI. The CIBI pledge is as follows:

> We are Afrikan people, struggling for national liberation. We are preparing leaders and workers to bring about positive change for our

> people. We stress the development of our bodies, minds, souls and consciousness. Our commitment is to self determination, self defense and self respect for our race.

These schools are filled with and have produced many positive role models. Many people involved in the independent school movement believe that in order to become more productive in the larger society, we as African-Americans must take time out to develop the self love, respect and esteem that was broken down during the American enslavement of Africans and that so many other cultures have and take for granted. This is a long and complicated process that needs to be completed. Many people interpret this period of completion as a separatist attitude. Further research on the parts of these critics would reveal a positive, self affirming attitude, which is necessary for the survival of any individual or group of people.

There are other schools of thought that suggest the best thing for African-American people to do is to take advantage of the established institutions, which happen to be predominantly white and have track records of success for the people that have been allowed to take advantage of them all along.

Not only is there controversy over the definition of progress, there is strong debate on what the path to progress should be. Carter G. Woodson (1933) writes about the need for service rather than leadership:

> . . . if we can finally succeed in translating the idea of leadership into that of service, we may soon find it possible to lift the Negro to a higher level. Under leadership we have come into the ghetto; by service within the ranks we may work our way out of it. Under leadership we have been constrained to do the biddings of others; by service we may work out a program in the light of our own circumstances. Under leadership we have become poverty stricken; by service we may teach the masses how to earn a living honestly. Under leadership we have been made to despise our own possibilities and develop into parasites; by service we may prove sufficient unto the task of self development and contribute our part to modern culture. (ppg. 118-119)

Woodson's writings illustrate that one way to get to the point of progress is through serving the community as opposed to simply leading or just discussing problems.

As discussed in chapter six, the way one defines oneself is directly related to the way one defines progress. When talking with the participants, we always discussed the goals of their activism. Each participant's goal gave an indication of what each saw as progress for the African-American community.

The goals of Hasani's activism relate to building institutions. He states:

> My basic philosophy is that I'm going to be an activist for life. And as an activist for life I am training my children to be activists, you see. I think that the preservation of a culture and the preservation of a people demands that we build institutions. You see I can stand on the corner and talk all day and say what I'm saying to you but nobody's gon' listen. But when you have institutions, when you have structures, okay. I mean everybody in the world has heard of the University of Chicago and everybody and they mama trying to get in there because that's supposed to be **the** university. And so we have to have institutions that are respected like that and listened to like that and that would be from cultural education . . . whatever institutions that a nation needs that's what we need and which means that if I come into a room to negotiate around anything, then you have a different level of respect.

Dr. Parker says that she has to get up every morning knowing that she has a purpose in this world. She discusses the idea of identity, purpose and direction; (Madhubuti, 1973, pg.33) knowing who you are, what you're here to do and what course to follow. Dr. Parker's overall goal is self-perfection. She believes that you improve your community by improving yourself. She admits that her goals are lofty and stresses that there must be balance. "We need to be working on self perfection but at the same time we need to be working to try to improve the things that affect our ability to perfect ourselves."

Of course perfection can be define in innumerable ways. The important thing is, as the term implies, each of us must define self-perfection for ourselves. This is part of our self-definition. Various groups may have theories that reflect the ideal state of the group. Christians may define the perfect Christian as one who obeys each of the Ten Commandments. Many in the Black nationalist community use the Nguzo Saba as the foundation for defining the ideal African-American community.

Factors That Affect Progress

Miseducation and Progress

Our inability as a people to think critically about and question our position in this world at any given time has ruled us defenseless and powerless in a political, technological, and historical world based upon defense and power. To be apolitical, atechnological and ahistorical (which by definition rules us inactive) in the Seventies is the highest compliment that can be paid to the effectiveness of the European American educational system. (Madhubuti, 1973, pg.143)

In Madhubuti's discussion, defenselessness and powerlessness are the result of miseducation. The lack of critical thinking is a central part of miseducation.

I believe that one the most harmful qualities of miseducation is its tenacity. Once individuals are miseducated, it seems they have the tendency to pass that miseducation on. Much of the miseducation of the African-American community is delivered through the very institutions that are looked to for real education; schools. Shujaa (1994) points out the distinction between education and schooling and asserts that "you can have one without the other." Shujaa further writes that " . . . African-Americans have long understood that schooling can both serve as well as betray their interests."

Miseducation can only be overcome if an individual or community as a whole realizes that they have been miseducated. This is no easy task since the miseducation process for the African-American has been extremely thorough as is indicated in Woodson's (1933) discussion of the control of a man's thinking.

> When You control a man's thinking, you do not have to control his actions. You do not have to tell him to stand here or go yonder. He will find his proper place and will stay in it. You do not need to send him to the back door. He will go without being told. In fact, if there is no back door, he will cut one for his special benefit. His education makes it necessary. (pg. xiii)

". . . His education makes it necessary." This is how deeply miseducated African-Americans have been, and are, in this country. A crucial element of miseducation is the lack of appreciation of the value of one's own culture. When one does not value one's own culture, it becomes very difficult to value oneself. If one does not value oneself, one's sense of ideal will likely be based on the values of some other culture. For many African-Americans who do not value African-American culture, European-American culture is usually the valued culture. When African-Americans place more value on European-American culture than their own, the things that are seen as ideal may not be to the benefit to the greatest number of African-Americans. The best standards for ideal for **any** group of people should be based primarily on the values of their own culture, since those values are formed with the well being of those people in mind. This has always been and may continue to be problematic for the culture in America in the numeric minority, especially for African-Americans. The involuntary manner in which African-Americans came to be in this country is a large part of what has caused the "psychic trauma" described by Latif and Latif (1994).

As were the vast majority of people of African descent in this country, each of the participants were miseducated. Each one of the participants, however, was able to rise above his or her miseducation.

Miseducation and the reeducation of oneself was certainly a central theme that emerged from the participant interviews. This issue was approached from several different angles but the premise upon which the need for re-education was based was generally the same; somehow, as African-Americans we have been mistaught and there is something problematic about the way we've been conditioned to think.

Barbara talks about miseducation:

> The worst thing in the world probably, and I say this with my name on this tape, is a European education. We have been taught that that is the best thing for us. If it is not balanced with something else, like somebody who is kind enough to give a child a book that tells the real story, you know, inside along with this so called training that takes place.

Barbara goes on to discuss a distinction that is made by Shujaa (1994): education versus schooling. Barbara says:

> I have a friend who will not use the word educated with regard to a formal institution. That you cannot be educated; you can only be trained. And I tend to believe that. That you learn some formulas, perhaps, for learning, but the learning, it depends on you. Most of our . . . I hate to be very careful about using these words, many of our Black teachers do not want to . . . there is denial and they simply will not address anything that is of African culture. And that is due to training.

Dr. Parker also speaks of this training that most people of African descent in America have experienced. She comments on how different African-Americans handle miseducation differently.

> I give alot of credence to the grace of God because much of what we do, in fact, more of what we do than what we don't do has to do with our fortune and misfortune. And I think there are people who the miseducation has taken a greater toll on than me. And you know, but for the grace of God, I would have been a person who would have been confused about my identity and would have identified with the white principal of the school rather than the Black teachers. Because the white principal of the school was all powerful.

Barbara and Dr. Parker speak of overcoming miseducation for some intangible kinds of reasons; true knowledge for truth's sake in Barbara's case and for the sake of a positive self concept, or identity, as discussed by Dr. Parker. Karimah talks about true education versus miseducation (subtly referred to as self education versus other education) in terms survival and progress of African-American people.

> And I guess one of the things I would say is that we need to take better care of ourselves on all those levels; mentally, physically and spiritually. Because the times that are coming up are going to be challenging times. You know there was a time when people could say, could talk about Affirmative Action and things like that. You talk Affirmative Action now and you not just talking about Black folks, you talking Viet Namese, Chinese, Arabs, you talking about everybody else and it makes it more competitive for us so our children should be educated. **Self education as well as other education**. I am really for setting up other kinds of schools and still sending to public schools but in our schools they will be taught who they are from an African-American perspective.

Some of the participants were fortunate enough to have been raised in an environment where the adults in the family were independent thinkers. However, each of them, at some point, either discovered that what they had been taught at American institutions was faulty or realized that something needed to be done with regard to the thinking of the African-American masses. Progress, then, comes both in the realization of the need for re-education and further in the re-education process itself.

For many of the participants, race consciousness came about only after a personal transformation took place. Certainly race is inextricably linked to personal consciousness but at different points in our lives other issues may come to the forefront. In *Makes Me Wanna Holler*, an autobiography of Nathan McCall, he writes that going through the divorce process was one of the most difficult things he's ever had to do and he believed that this was not race related. Part of becoming a strong contributor to the race is first developing a strong sense of self. Overcoming miseducation is the beginning of understanding oneself and going further to build a strong community.

Summary

The common quality in this group of participants was the willingness to put thought into action, Freire's concept of praxis. Each participant has definite ideas of what they see as progress for African-American people and further they are willing to make an active contribution to that progress.

The participants all had a concern for society as a whole, but each focused their activism on issues particularly relevant in the African-American community. I assert that the positive Black self concept each participant has is directly responsible for the approach that each has chosen to take with regard to his or her activism.

This chapter has outlined what the participants consider ideal for African-American people. I have included discussions on some of the major theories on progress and African-Americans and where these participants fit into these theories. I also outlined some of the factors that affect progress and how the participants overcame some of these obstacles.

In the next and final chapter, I will summarize all that has been learned from this research, why I took the approach that I did and possibilities for practical application of the findings.

Brennecke and Amick (1975) write that a good beginning to understanding and appreciating life fully is knowing that at some point it will end. Their discussion centers around human kind's struggle to make the time period between life's only two certainties, birth and death, meaningful and significant. They argue that human beings place far too much stress upon defining the purpose in and of our lives. They write, " our only purpose in life if 'purpose' is needed, is to be what we are fully, vitally and in a context of other people having the same right" (pg. 9) They do admit that to some extent we each need to find a purpose or goal in our existence but that we should not dwell on it.

I assert that Brennecke and Amick are far too idealistic in terms of the need for defining a life purpose. In a perfect world, each person being him or her self would be sufficient for a peaceful society. This theory breaks down when one individuals' selfhood conflicts with another's. We live in a world full of prejudices. In the current study, racism is the factor that dictates the need for African-Americans to define a purpose in life. Missing in Brennecke and Amick's discussion are the specific issues relevant to the lives of African-Americans that have an effect on the self.

VII
Conclusions

Introduction

Before discussing the implications of this research, it is necessary to revisit the questions with which this study began. There is one overall question from which several sub-questions have arisen.

This study is one of the narrated life experiences of 11 African-American intellectual-activists. The main question to be addressed in the data collection was what factors in the lives of these African-American men and women have moved them to the state of intellectual-activist. In addition to the variety of factors that may exist in the background of each participant, I wanted to know if there were any common threads that ran through the lives of those in the group. Although each of the participants fall into the category of intellectual-activist, each has a unique perspective. I wanted to delve into the diversity of perspectives that exist among the participants at hand. The diversity of perspectives manifests itself in the goals each participant has set for his or her activism and the purpose they have defined for their lives.

This final chapter will cover the implications in three major areas: the influence of nationalism on the lives of participants, the influence of religion on the lives of participants and the influence of the family structure on the lives of the participants. Each of these areas will be discussed within the context of African American self concept. Further, I will discuss expressions of positive African-American self concept, life purposes and progress toward life purposes among the participants.

Finally, the potential for practical application of my findings will be presented.

African-American Self Concept

This research started out as a study of the life histories of African-American nationalists. Part of the reason the participants were chosen was because either they define themselves as nationalists or are generally considered nationalists by others based on the groups with which they affiliate themselves, the kinds of activities in which they engage or the causes they champion. I quickly found that all participants did not feel comfortable with the Black Nationalist label. All agreed to some extent in the tenets of Black Nationalism, but most shunned the label. For this reason I felt it was important to write a chapter on self-definition. I found that part of the key to a worthwhile life history study is knowing how an individual defines him or herself. In this chapter I discussed the effects of African-American nationalism, religion and family on the self definitions of the participants. I went on to discuss the turning points in their lives that put them on the course to their present philosophies.

The influence of religion on the lives of the participants.

My research revealed that African-American intellectuals who subscribe to nationalist tenets are moving towards a more general spirituality and away from organized religion.

Each of the participants has been exposed to the African-American church. In fact, the church was an integral part of the lives of most of the participants. Frazier (1957) writes:

> So important has been the Negro church in the life of the Negro in the South that the Negro population has been divided into two large religious communities- Baptists and Methodists. Consequently the Negro church has provided the arena for the political struggles of a

> people shut out from the political life of the American community. (pg. 78)

Frazier (1957) goes on to discuss the importance of the church in other aspects of African-American life such as voting rights and union membership. Frazier's notions reflect the feelings of many African-Americans today in that the church is the center of the community and that it should be actively involved in finding solutions to the present day ills that challenge this community. John Drew made that point throughout his interview with me. For example:

> And for the most part I think that the people who are making things happen, both positively and negatively in the neighborhoods, are doing it through the churches.

John feels very strongly about the responsibility of the church to facilitate change in the African American community. However, most of the participants would not concur.

The majority of the participants want positive change to occur from whatever source it can occur, but, they personally place very little stock in organized religion in terms of their own spiritual development and their development as intellectual-activists.

On several different occasions throughout the data, the word hypocrisy was used by participants with regard to organized religion. This is all very relevant in that it refutes both popular belief and much of the literature in terms of the influence of the organized church in the lives of successful African-Americans.

My findings are more in line with Asante (1988) who discusses the notion of the organized church as being both a help and a hinderance in the African-American community.

The influence of family structure on the lives of the participants.

The importance of a strong family unit to the mental, physical and spiritual health of a child is a concept that is not unique to the African-American community. The nuclear family is still seen by many as the ideal family structure. My research indicates not that the nuclear family isn't the ideal structure, but that it is not a prerequisite to a prosperous and healthy life.

The participants in this study were raised in a variety of family settings. Several in the nuclear family with married parents present in the home. Several of my participants were raised in extended family environments with mother, father, grandparents, aunts and uncles. Some were raised by grandparents, one by an aunt, one in foster care and one essentially raised himself. There were single fathers and mothers among the structures. This truly represents the gamut in terms of family structure. There was variety in the input, but consistency in the output; African-American people who possess a positive self concept. This particular finding is especially controversial in the wake of America's public political discussion on family values.

The observation that children do well without the traditional American family structure is not to be used as an excuse for deadbeat moms or dads. One implication of this finding is that there is no need to automatically write off the boy from the fatherless home as a future hopeless man.

The other issue at hand is that not only do my participants have a positive self concept, they each have a positive African-American self concept. The difference is that the first does not imply the second. An African-American could very well feel good about him or her self as a parent, as a member of his or her profession or a man or woman and still feel insecurity or bitterness with regard to his or her status as an African-American.

One way to identify a person's insecurity as an African-American is by observing excessive negative references to people of other races.These participants were centered in their African-American-ness. Their collective concern was with aggressively addressing the challenges within the African-American community as opposed spending an inordinate amount of time placing blame. This kind of confidence and centeredness came from each of my well rounded, well adjusted participants. There is consensus within their interviews that each is happy and proud to be of African descent. Although each is able to acknowledge the challenges faced by Africans and African-Americans, thus the need for their activism, each maintains a positive attitude with regard to the African-American community. Although this adjustment is not solely due to upbringing, much of it is. Some of the participants were raised by African-American nationalists so nationalist tenets, which stress the importance of family and community, were taught directly. Most of them were raised by people who taught them, in their own way, to be critical thinkers. Therefore, they grew up to be critical thinkers and made decisions based on those thoughts that led them to accept the tenets of African-American nationalism that encourage independence and freedom for people of African descent. Either way, the family, regardless of how it was defined, had a positive effect on the lives of the participants.

Expressions of Positive African-American Self Concept

Aside from the contributing factors, such as religion, spirituality and the family to the development of a positive African-American self concept, another interesting finding is in terms of the ways in which the participants chose to outwardly express that positive African-American self concept.

I found that as a group, it was important to the participants to somehow make a public statement with regard to their concepts of themselves as African-Americans. They made this statement in two major ways: Afrocentric appearance, which includes hair and attire and African names.

There was only one participant in the group who I never saw in African garments. This does not, however, mean that he does not wear African garments. This particular participant, John, was the one that I saw the least outside of the formal interview setting. In fact, I only saw him one time outside of the interview setting and that was the day that I met him. We spoke several times on the telephone. Other than John, the remainder of the participants regularly dress in African garments. I found that an interesting comparison was one between those who regularly wore African garments to those whose hair was worn in a natural style, to those who used African names. There was some inconsistency there.

If I were to rank the expressions of Afrocentricity in terms of permanence, I would rank a legal name change as most permanent, a natural hairstyle next and African attire as the least permanent form of expression. I am ranking clothing the least permanent because it can be changed most readily and most often. The hairstyle applies more to the female participants since issues and standards of beauty were raised far more often among them. I would rank the natural hairstyle second most permanent because although it can be changed, the change was made less frequently than changes in attire. For example, over the two years that these data were collected, I have seen the participants in an out of African attire where the state of hair remained relatively consistent. Female participants may have changed form one natural hair style to another, but the styles were generally free of chemicals. The use of an African name had several degrees: non use, use only in the cultural community, consistent use in all spheres of the public except legally, and the legal name change.

So, given the levels of permanence of expressions of Afrocentricity, an interesting point is raised considering that the most common form of expression of Afrocentricity among the participants was the least permanent, according to my rankings; African attire. The question then becomes, why, among this group of individuals with a commitment to, love and respect for the African-American culture and strong affiliation with the African-American nationalist community, is there not more consistency in the use of the more permanent expressions of Afrocentricity.

I will not challenge the level of commitment these participants have to the African-American community. My conclusion is that although the verbal expression of a positive African-American self concept is high, there is still some level of desire for acceptance by the African-American masses and the society at large. Karima has given testimony to knowing the proper time to dress in African attire. Barbara has said that she has an African name but does not use it in public. Fatima uses her African name regularly but has not taken steps to change it legally so that they may be used with complete consistency. Hasani, talks about the power he feels walking into a room with an African name but still uses his birth name on particular occasions. Hakim uses his birth name in many of the articles that he has had printed. These are examples of the inconsistencies taking place within the lives of the participants. Even in the face of these inconsistencies, I maintain that they are getting the job done in terms of increasing the life chances of many of the girls and boys with whom they come into contact. In the next section I discuss the conclusions I have reached about the progress they are making.

Life Purposes and Progress

I found, with the participants, that all had the general goal of the uplift of African-American people. What differed is what is considered uplift. One participant is convinced that possession of economic independence and an entrepreneurial spirit is the epitome of uplift. The same participant saw the church as a major player in making this possible.

Most participants somehow saw children as the best chance for guaranteeing the uplift of the race. Many of the participants teach children directly or teach teachers of children. The slogan that the children are our future has probably been adopted by most cultures. This could be considered factual since children literally are the future of this and all nations. In twenty or thirty years, today's children will be the decision makers for our society. There is almost a desperate tone, however, to the voices of the participants who place supreme value on training our children to become conscious and active regarding the struggle of African-American people. It is as if they believe our only possible chance at survival as a race is our future generations.

I believe that progress for African-American people will only come when African-American people begin to take action. Before action is taken, the problem should be well defined, well researched, either through formal academic studies or grass roots observations, well planned and well tested and evaluated. This is not an easy process. This dissertation is merely one portion of my personal action plan. I have several ideas as to how this idea can be translated into action and these words into work. In the next section, I will demonstrate the way this data can be used to brainstorm about practical applications.

Practical Applications

In the case of the participants in this study, self concept was often a result of one or more turning points in their lives. One of the turning points in my short life was my move to Chicago. For me, then 26, it was a statement of independence. Although I haven't lived with my parents on a full time basis for nearly 10 years, changing cities was the exhilarating step that I needed to take in order to feel truly independent. I planned it for over a year, but nothing could have prepared me for the feeling I had as my Nova and I scooted along I-90 West in search of a new life. I leaned out of my car window to take a one-handed picture of the sign that read "Welcome to Illinois." And in keeping with the tradition of me, I wept at the sight of the sign that read "Welcome to Chicago." I was finally here, wherever here was. Even though my parents raised me to be an independent person; to live on my own, work hard and take care of my financial affairs, for the first time in my life, my ***spirit*** felt free. This was a decision that I had made without regard to anyone but myself. I had made a change in my life, for me and about me. I didn't concern myself with what people would think or how they would feel. But this was not a selfish move. It was a gift from me to me. The gift of power over my own life. This was my opportunity to define myself for myself. This was a critical point in my personal transformation.

Each of the participants relayed one or more experiences to me that they believed changed the courses of their lives. In these discussions is where I found the potential for practical application. Their turnings points included the birth of a child, meeting a spouse for the first time, hearing a speech, reading a book, divorce, a spiritual experience, getting through to a student, graduation from a university, and experiences in military service. Although turning points can be negative, the ones on which I focussed were positive.

West (1990) discussed the concept of a conversion like experience that leads people to commit their lives to intellectual activities for the purposes of pleasure, personal growth and political enhancement of one's people. This notion played itself out during the course of my interviews with the participants. On the whole, the transformation to intellectual-activist was described as a slow but steady evolution that included multiple episodes of sudden enlightenment. The overall process was gradual but on many occasions during the process, participants may have read a book or heard a speech or had a conversation that renewed their enthusiasm and provided them with assurance that they were on the right path.

Kwame was an example of an participant with mis-channelled energy. He took questionable actions to satisfy legitimate desires. Today he is successful and dedicated to positivity and the education of African-American children. Left to his own devices, he may have been counted among the Black male prison statistics. He is living testimony to the possibility of change and the power of personal transformation. It is important to look at young men and women whose actions may be immoral or illegal but whose skills might have been commended or even coveted under other circumstances. For example, an eight year old who is able to persuade otherwise upstanding friends to steal candy may have the makings of a class president or in later life, a salesman or motivational speaker. After all, the skill needed is the art of persuasion. Instead of simply criticizing the actions of our youngsters, we should move towards constructive criticism and develop programs designed to assist them in recognizing their own skills and positive ways in which these talents might be used.

Fatima is also an example of an participant who demonstrated the capacity for change and the power of personal transformation. As a teenager she was into hard drugs. Reading an autobiography of Malcolm

X, was one of the things that began to help her realize that rebellion doesn't need to have a negative connotation.

This research is really all about practical applications. It's about looking for what worked in the lives of successful men and women and creating programs using the results of the research as philosophies that guide these programs.

When I talk about successful men and women, it is not about financial success. In fact, none of the participants in this study live particularly extravagant lifestyles. I consider them successful primarily because the made a commitment to the present and future of African and African-American people and more importantly, they are seeing that commitment through.

There is something about the African-American struggle that is sad but at the same time wonderful and that is that the struggle never ends. The concept that our struggle is eternal is somewhat overwhelming and even depressing and that makes it sad. But because the struggle is never ending, its never too late to join. As Kwame says:

> Some people might get turned on by a book, some people might get turned on by a speaker, I don't care when it happens or how it happens, just as long as it happens, I say RIGHT ON !

Right on to a positive Black self concept (identity). Right on to defining a life purpose that includes goals that uplift of African-American people (purpose) and right on to making moves toward those goals (direction). This is the essence of African-American Intellectual-Activism.

References

Akbar, N. (1982). *From Miseducation to Education.* Jersey City, NJ: New Mind Productions.

Akoto, K.A. (1973). *Nationbuilding: theory and practice in Afrikan-centered education.* Washington, DC: Pan Afrikan World Institute.

Ani, M. (1994). *Yurugu.* Trenton, NJ: Africa World Press.

Argyle, F. (1968). *The self concept of Negro and white school beginners.* Paper presented at the Annual Meeting of the American Educational Research Association.

Asante, M.K. (1988). *Afrocentricity.* Trenton, NJ: Africa World Press.

Asante, M.K. and Asante, K.W. (1985). *African Culture: the rhythms of unity.* Westport, CT: Greenwood Press.

Bertaux, D. (ed.) (1981). *Biography and Society: the life history approach in the social sciences.* Beverly Hills, CA: International Sociological Association.

Bogdan, R. and Biklen, S. (1982). *Qualitative Research for Education: an introduction to theory and methods.* Boston: Allyn and Bacon, Inc.

Bracey, J.H., Meier, A and Rudwick, E. (eds.) (1970). *Black Nationalism in America.* Indianapolis: The Bobbs-Merrill Company, Inc.

Brennecke, J. and Amick, R. (1975). *The Struggle for Significance.* Encino, CA: Glencoe Publishing Co, Inc.

Brennecke, J. and Amick, R. (1980). *Significance: the struggle we share.* Encino, CA: Glenco Publishing Co, Inc.

Castenell, L. and Pinar, W. (eds.) (1993). *Understanding Curriculum as Racial Text.* Albany: State University of New York Press.

Clarke, J.H. (1991). *Notes for an African World Revolution: Africans at the crossroads.* Trenton, NJ: Africa World Press.

Cruse, H. (1967). *The Crisis of the Negro Intellectual.* New York: William Morrow and Company, Inc.

Denzin, N.K. (1970). *The Research Act: a theoretical introduction to sociological methods*. Chicago: Aldine Publishing Company.

DuBois, W.E.B. (1961). *Souls of Black Folk*. Greenwich: Fawcett.

Edwards, A. and Polite, C. (1992). *Children of the Dream: the psychology of Black success*. New York: Doubleday.

Fanon, F. (1963). *The Wretched of the Earth*. New York: Grove Press.

Foster, H.J. (1983). African Patterns in the Afro-American Family. *Journal of Black Studies*. Vol. 14. No. 2.

Frazier, E.F. (1949). *The Negro in the United States*. New York: The McMillan Company.

Frazier, E.F. (1962). *Black Bourgeoisie*. New York: The Free Press.

Frazier, E.F. (1966). *The Negro Family in the United States*. Chicago: University of Chicago Press.

Frazier, E.F. (1968). *On Race Relations*. Chicago: University of Chicago Press.

Frazier, E.F. (1973). The Failure of the Negro Intellectual. (written in 1962). In Joyce A. Ladner (ed.) *The Death of a White Sociology*. (pp. 52-66). New York: Random House.

Freire, P. (1970). *Pedagogy of the Oppressed*. New York: Herder and Herder.

Freire, P. (1973). *Education for a Critical Consciousness*. New York: Seabury Press.

Gordon, B. (1990). The Necessity of African-American Epistemology for Educational Theory and Practice. In *Journal of Education*. Vol. 172, No. 3. Boston: Boston Unuversity.

Gordon, V. (1976). The Methodologies of Black Self Concept Research: a critique. In *Journal of Afri-American Issues*. Vol. IV. Numbers 3-4, Summer/Fall.

Greene, M. (1978). *Landscapes of Learning*. New York: Teachers College Press.

Guinea-Bissau: Toward final victory: selected speeches and documents from PAIGC (Partido Africano da Independencia da Guine e Cabo Verde). Richmond, BC, Canada: LSM Information Center, 1974.

Hewitt, John P. (1989). *Dilemmas of the American Self*. Philadelphia: Temple University Press.

Karenga, M. (1988). *The African American Holiday of Kwanzaa: a celebration of family, community and culture*. Los Angeles, CA: University of Sankore Press.

Karenga, M. (1985). The African Intellectual and the Problem of Class Suicide: Ideological and political dimensions. In Molefi Asante and Kariamu Welsh-Asante (eds.) *African Culture: the rhythms of unity*. Westport, CT: Greenwood Press.

Kunjufu, J. (1988). *Countering the Conspiracy to Destroy Black Boys*. Chicago: Afro-Am Publishers.

Latif, N and Latif, S. (1994). *Slavery: The African-American Psychic Trauma*. Chicago: Latif Communications Group, Inc.

Linde, C. (1989). "Narrative in Conversation." In preparation for *Oxford Encyclopedia of Linguistics*: Edited by William Bright, et al, Oxford University Press.

Littlejohn-Blake, S. and Darling, C. (1993). Understanding the Strengths of African-American Families. *Journal of Black Studies*. Vol. 4 No. 3.

Lynch, H.R. (1971). *Black Spokesman: selected published writings of E.W. Blyden*. London: Frank Cass and Company Limited.

Madhubuti, H.R. (1973). *From Plan to Planet, Life Studies: the need for Afrikan minds and institutions*. Chicago: Third World Press.

Madhubuti, H.R. (1978). *Enemies: the clash of the races*. Chicago: Third World Press.

Madhubuti, H.R. (1990). *Black Men: Obsolete, Single and Dangerous? Afrikan American families in transition: essays in discoveries, solutions and hope*. Chicago: Third World Press.

Mead, G. (1934). *Mind, Self ans Society: from the standpoint of the social behaviorist*. Chicago: University of Chicago Press.

Moss, W. W. (1974). *Oral History Program Manual*. New York: Praeger Publishers.

The Negro Problem: a series of articles by representative Negroes of today. Miami: Mnemosyne Publishing Inc., 1969.

Ritzer, G. (1988). *Sociological Theory (second edition)*. New York: Alfred A Knopf Inc.

Rodney, W. (1990). *Walter Rodney Speaks: the making of an African intellectual*. Trenton, NJ: Africa World Press.

Scott, K.Y. (1991). *The Habit of Surviving*. New York: Ballantine Books.

Shujaa, M.J. (1994). *Too Much Schooling, Too Little Education*. Trenton, NJ: Africa World Press.

Shujaa, M.J. (1993). "Education and Schooling: You can have one without the other" in *Urban Education*, Vol. 27 No. 4.

Spradley, J. (1979). *The Ethnographic Interview*. Orlando, FL: Holt, Rinehart and Winston, Inc.

Stanfield, J.H and Dennis, R.M. (eds.) (1993). *Race andEthnicity in Research Methods*. Newbury Park: Sage Publications.

Stryker, S. (1980). *Symbolic Interactionism*. Menlo Park, CA: Benjamin/Cummings Publishing Company, Inc.

Washington, B.T. (1899). *The Future of the American Negro.* Boston: Small, Maynard and Company.

Weinberg, M. (ed.) (1970). *W.E.B. DuBois: A reader.* New York: Harper and Row Publishers.

West, C. (1993). *Race Matters.* New York: Vintage Books.

West, C. and hooks, b. (1991). *Breaking Bread: insurgent Black intellectual life.* Boston: South End Press.

Woodson, C.G. (1990, 1933). *The Miseducation of the Negro.* Trenton, NJ: Africa World Press.

Wyne, M. (1974). *The Black Self.* Englewood Cliffs, NJ: Prentice-Hall Inc.

Index